PARTITION LAWSUIT:

LESSONS LEARNED

PARTITION LAWSUIT:

LESSONS LEARNED

Stephanie Siddall Germack, Ph.D., NCC, LPC

Publisher: Stephanie Siddall Germack

ISBN 978-1515124542

Grateful Thanks and Prayers

I offer thanks to our Father in Heaven for His guidance and direction. Thank you, Lord, for giving me the strength to persevere and to follow the path that You have chosen for me to follow.

Thanks to my husband, Jim and my son, Jason for their never-wavering love, support, patience and understanding.

Dedication

I dedicate this book to the memory of my late mother, Mary Courter Siddall (February 15, 1915 – April 29, 2011).

Table of Contents

The Definition of Witness and Exhibit List

Plaintiffs' Attorney's Witness and Exhibit List

Defendants' Witness and Exhibit List

Defendants' Rationale for Filing Witness and Exhibit List

New Terms: Evidence, Discovery

Defendants' Concerns to Date

New Participants: Ms. Low Appraiser, Ms. High Appraiser

Defendants Have Appraisals Completed

The Definition of Appraisal

Defendants Receive Results of One Appraisal

Defendants' Purpose of Obtaining Appraisal

First Reason the Case Took Years to Complete

Plaintiffs' Purpose of Obtaining Appraisal
Ordered by Judge
To Sell the Property

Plaintiffs' Appraisal Completed

Chapter VI – Mediation

Why Choose Mediation?

The Definitions of Mediation and Arbitration

Recommended Questions to Ask at a Mediation

Negotiating Techniques

New Participants: Ms. Mediator, Mr. Mediator

Mediation Hearing

Plaintiffs Technically Had Already Refused Mediation

Plaintiffs Refuse to Attend

Plaintiffs Agree to Mediation Only for Appearances

Plaintiffs' Refusal to Negotiate

Plaintiffs' Attorney's Requests

Plaintiffs' Attorney Rejects Ms. Low Appraiser's Appraisal

Mediators' Recommendations to Defendant

Plaintiffs' Terms from Defendants' Perspective

Plaintiffs Hadn't Considered Odds of Winning, Bottom Line, Options, or Time Spent Negotiating

The Serenity Prayer

Author Biography

PARTITION LAWSUIT:

LESSONS LEARNED

Stephanie Siddall Germack, Ph.D., NCC, LPC

Introduction

*I have changed names and some details for the purpose of this book to protect the innocent.

A partition lawsuit is one of several legal actions that a layperson likely does not have awareness until he or she is either the initiator, the individual sued, or a bystander. Since a partition is a legal action, the individuals who are most and best informed are attorneys. As many lawyers will agree, a partition can be a lengthy and costly process. And most attorneys recommend that partition only be used as the last resort when all other options have been discussed and have failed.

Once this type of lawsuit is filed, many individuals assume that extensive discussion has already taken place between the parties involved. Often partition cases are settled within a couple of weeks without court involvement for that reason. The discussion has taken place. And, as a result, the parties involved avoid costly legal proceedings, the need to hire attorneys, and lengthy, often highly emotional, distressing, and exhausting courtroom experiences.

However, there are those who completely refuse discussion about non-legal, creative options prior to filing lawsuits. Although filing a partition lawsuit is the most extreme option used to divide property, some individuals still choose legal action over simple face-to-face discussions regardless of the costs and potential damage to the family structure. That is the basis of this story.

As I began to research information about partition lawsuits, I found some postings written by attorneys in explanation of basic terms and general facts about partition. However, I was unable to find key information about why partition lawsuits take so long to complete. I also had hoped to find more information about the partition legal process available to the general public. For additional reference, I looked for case studies to learn how individuals dealt with their situations particularly where the partition lawsuit involved blood relatives as opposed to other types of partition lawsuits. The case studies that I found were non-scientific authors' accountings of individuals' stories of rejection by family members related to numerous situations. In the majority of cases, the family target was neither aware of the cause for the rejection nor responsible (Folberg, 2009).

My purpose in writing this book is to provide information to the general public about the basic procedure of a partition lawsuit, some of the techniques that I've observed that attorneys use in adversarial cases, and the situations that one might face if involved in a partition lawsuit with family members.

I present this accounting from a defendant's and layperson's point of view with the general goal that plaintiffs can avoid the challenges inherent to partition by choosing non-legal options toward settlement.

I've based this story on an actual partition lawsuit between blood relatives, however with names and a range of other details changed. The story is based on factual events. I have attempted to restrain from exaggerating facts and behaviors so that the reader will be better able to compare the extremes of this case with his or her family's situation or other cases.

I've told the story in sequential order of the events. In some instances, I've added definitions and comments to clarify events before they occurred. I hope that this format helps the reader to better understand both the legal aspects of a partition lawsuit and the psychological elements involved in experiencing the process from the defendant's point of view.

I've included descriptions of the characteristics that are common to family structures particularly in dysfunctional families in which communication is lacking. General topics that include bullying, sibling rivalry, narcissism, and sociopathic behaviors may help the reader to understand the range of reasons related to how and why individuals choose to refuse discussion with family members.

Finally, I present a list of points that in the opinion of this author, serve as lessons learned. While interpretations play a large part in whether or not lawyers and laypeople view actions as mistakes, when the consequences involve financial waste and broken relationships, common sense dictates the choice of alternative options that lead to Win-Win solutions.

Chapter I – Background – This Partition Lawsuit

Disclaimer: I am not a lawyer. The reader should not interpret any statements within this book as legal advice under any circumstances. The basis for this story is one unique lawsuit. The reader should not assume that this accounting is representative of any other partition lawsuits.

To understand the reasons to settle with non-legal options as opposed to filing a partition lawsuit even when one or more co-owners no longer want to own a property, it is helpful to learn the specifics about partition first. Knowledge is critical to distinguishing the challenges of a lawsuit. Many may assume that filing a lawsuit is the only way to resolve a perceived disagreement over ownership of real estate. And they might also assume that discussion has taken place if the initiators have filed a lawsuit. However, that is not always the case. In this story, the plaintiffs refused discussion with their siblings prior to their filing the lawsuit. By refusing discussion, the plaintiffs initiated a process that was financially costly and wasteful to all of the co-owners, but particularly to them. Had the plaintiffs chosen to discuss multiple options with their siblings prior to or immediately after they filed their lawsuit, the property may have been saved and relationships renewed.

The Definition of Partition

The definition of *partition* (Partition, USLegal.com, 2015) is: "The dividing of lands held by joint tenants into distinct portions so that they may hold them in severalty . . . Partition provides a method whereby two or more persons who own property together may put an end to their joint ownership, so that each may own a separate portion of the property or, if a division in kind is not feasible, the property may be sold, and each owner given an appropriate share of the proceeds."

The types of a partition are *judicial* or *voluntary*. In judicial partitions the court becomes involved when the owners cannot agree to sell the property; in such cases, any one owner can file a partition lawsuit against one or more of the other owners to force a sale of the property. In voluntary partitions, the owners agree among themselves to sell and exchange deeds (Partition, USLegal.com, 2015).

Partition in kind, or actual partition occurs when the property is divided among the owners in such a way that each owner can "continue to enjoy his or her share of the property and can also dispose of his or her share without any obstruction from the other owners" (Partition, USLegal.com, 2015). If the property cannot be divided into physical parts, then a partition by sale takes place. A judge orders the sale of the property; the proceeds are divided between the owners depending on the percentage of each owner's share.

"The court may refuse to grant partition only in extreme cases" (Partition, USLegal.com, 2015). In most, if not all states, an individual is not forced to own property. Partition is, therefore, an option to use to divide the property or dissolve ownership interests.

TheFreeDictionary.com (Partition, 2015) further offers, "A tenant in common or a joint tenant has the absolute right to seek a compulsory partition. Partition must be made even if every other owner objects to it. The motives of the party seeking partition are irrelevant, and the court that hears the lawsuit has no discretion to deny partition. Its main function is to determine the method of executing the partition."

Those are the legal definitions of a partition. One might assume from reading the definitions that filing a lawsuit results in a simple, quick conclusion; the property is sold within a few weeks. However, the reality is that a lawsuit case can become disturbingly complicated, taking years to complete even when non-contested.

None of the definitions address the questions: How is a partition lawsuit costly? Why is a partition lawsuit lengthy? Can a property be saved once a lawsuit has been filed? Will filing a partition lawsuit destroy family relationships?

Let's begin by discussing the initial potential costs of a partition lawsuit and a possible root of dissension.

There are numerous individuals who may become involved in partition lawsuits. First, there are the plaintiffs, the co-owners who file lawsuits; plaintiffs often hire attorneys to file their lawsuits and to argue for partitions. Next, there are the defendants, the co-owners against whom the lawsuits are filed. Defendants might or might not hire attorneys, sometimes preferring to act as their legal counsel or acting *pro se*. Depending on the case and the parties' preferences, "Co-owners may select an arbitrator or appraiser to divide the property and to allot shares" (Partition, TheFreeDictionary.com, 2015). Sometimes a "special master (referee or receiver) … who reports to the court and may employ professionals (engineers, surveyors and other experts) is appointed by the court" (Partition (law), 2015). A range of other individuals might also be hired, including insurance agents, real estate appraisers, realtors, and property inspectors. Each of these individual charges a fee, and in many cases, each individual also works with an attorney. Additional individuals hired might include those who maintain the property such as roofers, construction experts, and lawn maintenance workers. Further costs can include court costs, mailing fees, transcript fees, etc. All of those fees are charged to the co-owners, including the attorney fees of third parties, appraisers, realtors, roofers, and all other hired individuals.

In this lawsuit, the plaintiffs demanded payment for their attorney fees and all costs by the defendants although the plaintiffs had not had any prior face-to-face discussions with their sibling co-owners about the property.

Caught off-guard, the defendants would learn the legal process as the case continued.

Three Required Procedures - Notice, Appraisal, Right of First Refusal

A website that addresses the partition procedure is http://www.Uniformlaws.org. It summarizes the Partition of Heirs Property Act. According to that site, there are three steps to completing a partition: notice, appraisal, and right of first refusal (Partition of Heirs Property Act Summary, 2015).

Although the three-step procedure probably satisfies the legal requirements of a case, it doesn't address the additional procedures for mediation, negotiation and the multitude of other creative ways for settling a case.

One might believe that the three steps take only weeks or months to complete. On the contrary, the actual procedure can take years even in a non-contested case. There are multiple reasons that a partition lawsuit can take years to complete that include the filing of motions and legal documents, court procedures, hearings, and a range of other factors influenced by the initiating participants.

Participants

Plaintiffs

The plaintiffs are three members of one family of birth.

Marta – Age: 57, primary initiator of the lawsuit

Barbara – Age: 67

Debra – Age: 71

Defendants

The defendants are the plaintiffs' two siblings by blood.

Rebecca – Age: 58

William – Age: 63

Plaintiffs' Attorney

Mr. Plaintiffs' Attorney

Judge (Heard all but the final hearing)

The Honorable Mr. Impartial

Subject of Lawsuit

The five siblings inherited their parent's summer-vacation residence when their parent passed. The residence had been in the family for 80 years and had been enjoyed previously by four generations, all of whom worked together, cooperated so that all enjoyed the property by sharing tasks to maintain it and contributing to the common good. The five siblings are each equal, one-fifth owners of the property.

Family Dynamics: Bullying, Sibling Rivalry, Control, Disagreement over Care of Aging Parent

Prior to the filing of the lawsuit, the siblings seemed to enjoy their relationships with each other, although there had been isolated displays of sibling rivalry, particularly between the two youngest siblings and between the two older middle siblings earlier in their lives. As their one living parent aged, the two sets of siblings' differences seemed to escalate as issues of bullying, sibling rivalry, and control increased.

Although the siblings' personalities were radically different, they, as children, spent many happy years together. Once they reached adulthood, they rarely spent time with each other but kept in regular contact, either by visiting on holidays or by telephone. Except for the occasional simple disagreement, the siblings rarely fought. They instead usually kept their differences to themselves.

The first indication of extreme discord came when their remaining living parent reached the age of 85. In a move that surprised everyone, the youngest sibling, Marta, and one of the middle siblings, Barbara forced their parent into the probate court without having discussed this with their parent, Rebecca, William, or Debra. Their parent was without physical or cognitive health challenges at the time of the probate court action. While Marta and Barbara seemed to view their action as a righteous attempt to "save" their parent by forcing residence in an assisted-care facility, to their siblings, the fact that these two instigators had excluded the rest of the family from a discussion of their plans belied other motives. The other siblings simply did not understand what reasons there could be for any, let alone total, secrecy.

In the months immediately following their probate legal action, Marta and Barbara persuaded Debra to join their alliance by gifting her with some of their parent's possessions prior to their parent's passing, an action that their siblings later witnessed and confirmed during a probate court hearing that all five siblings attended. Debra continued to periodically telephone both Rebecca and William. Neither foresaw that Debra would eventually suddenly also cut off communication with Rebecca and William.

Marta, Barbara, and Debra seemed unconcerned with their parent's pleas to leave the assisted care facility and return to live in either of their parent's homes depending on the season. Through the Guardian, the three sisters dismissed Rebecca's and William's suggestions of ways to improve their parent's quality of life.

And they showed little empathy toward their siblings' desire to visit their parent. They had set up an adversarial process in which Rebecca and William had been assigned the role of adversaries without Rebecca's or William's prior knowledge. The only way that Rebecca or William could have changed their assigned roles would have been to unconditionally join forces with their siblings, agree with whatever their plan was without complaint, and allow their siblings to lead regardless of the cost to their parent or themselves.

Marta's and Barbara's attorney fees were paid from their parent's estate as were all other costs and payments to the guardians, Conservator, and their attorneys. As a result, their action against their parent cost them little if any money.

Rebecca and William assumed that Marta's and Barbara's lack of communication was due to their probate-court action. Perhaps their attorney had advised them not to communicate with their siblings as part of the adversarial process. They had no idea of the reasons behind their siblings' refusal to talk with them. Although years before, the two had met with Rebecca, William, and the opposing attorneys for an agreement meeting, Marta and Barbara had reneged on their terms of the mutual agreement only two weeks later. While one sister feigned cooperation, the other demonstrated brewing anger. But both kept the reasons for their emotions to themselves.

With the exception of Marta's and Barbara's action of beginning to remove small items from their parent's homes, and the continuation of a variety of allegations by Marta and Barbara against their siblings, there had been no other event that had occurred, no heated argument, nothing even slightly confrontational that had happened prior to Marta's and Barbara's probate-court action. This extreme action was completely out of the blue.

Although the Conservator sold their parent's winter residence several years before their parent's passing, he was unable to sell the summer residence which had been protected due to its location in a different state. Also the residence was held by a trust that had been set up by the siblings' grandparents for their parent's benefit.

The summer residence had been in the family for 80 years. Despite the sibling discord that Rebecca and William observed, they still thought that their siblings loved the summer residence. After all, as a family they had spent many summers together in carefree appreciation of nature and their immediate relatives. There were laughter and good spirits every day with tasks shared toward the common good of all who visited. An idyllic place, the siblings enjoyed every minute at their parent's lakefront home.

So Marta's, Barbara's, and Debra's partition lawsuit came as a second unexpected surprise to Rebecca and William. Both were shocked that their siblings would file a lawsuit against them without having had any face-to-face discussion at all.

Chapter II – Summons and Complaint

The Definition of Summons and Complaint

A *Summons and Complaint* is a legal document used to give notice to defendants about a lawsuit. Depending on the state in which the lawsuit is filed, the first page of the document specifically states, "You are being sued. You have 21 days after receiving this summons to file a written answer with the court and serve a copy on the other party or take other lawful action with the court (28 days if you were served by mail or you were served outside this state). If you do not answer or take other action within the time allowed, judgment may be entered against you for the relief demanded in the complaint" (Summons and Complaint, 2012).

Plaintiffs' Attorney's Statements in Summons and Complaint

Mr. Plaintiffs' Attorney had prepared the Summons and Complaint. The next four pages included statements regarding percentage of ownership of the property, followed by legal terms related to the court's jurisdiction to partition and order the sale of the property, the county in which the property is located, and additional court jurisdiction over the plaintiffs and defendants.

A section entitled "General Allegations" included information about the siblings' parent's previous ownership of the property through the trust, and additional information pertaining to how, when, and from whom the property deeds were transferred to the five owners.

Then, under a new section, entitled "Partition", Mr. Plaintiffs' Attorney stated additional information about the plaintiffs and defendants as the only five co-owners of the property.

And the final section of the document requested that the court grant different forms of relief, either a partition or sale of the property and the appointment of a Receiver to "lease and manage the property", that the plaintiffs recover their costs including attorney fees, and additional information.

Defendants' Perspective

Defendants' Questions – Legal

Rebecca received the hand-delivered Summons and Complaint on June 10, 2012. According to the date entered on the document, her sisters had filed the lawsuit on April 23, 2012. The delay in delivery was due to typographical error within Rebecca's address.

Her first reaction to receiving the document was shock. She read through the document several times before telephoning William. Although listed as the first defendant, he had not yet received his copy of the document. There was no explanation for that delay.

The topic of partition was for the most part, completely new to both Rebecca and William. So, they began to gather as much information as possible. With use of the Internet, Rebecca and William studied terms related to partition. They needed to become familiar with the legal procedure, the process, and the roles that different individuals play.

Not knowing what to expect, Rebecca and William developed a list of questions.

How would a Receiver lease and manage the property and what would be the cost? Since the buildings needed new roofs and minor repair, the property could not realistically be leased to a third party.

Did Mr. Plaintiffs' Attorney mean that the plaintiffs intended to lease the property to Rebecca and William even though they are co-owners? Rebecca and William didn't know. As equal co-owners, Rebecca and William had as much right to use the property as did the plaintiffs.

Was it standard legal procedure to include the plaintiffs' claim that the defendants pay the plaintiffs' attorney fees? Or was it a specific course of action that Marta, Barbara, and Debra had specifically requested that Mr. Plaintiffs' Attorney follow? If the action was the latter, it would suggest specific aggression against the defendants who were unsuspecting targets.

The majority of the statements in the Summons and Complaint were factual information most that described ownership of the property.

However, one particular statement toward the end of the document took on the characteristic of opinion rather than fact. Since Mr. Plaintiffs' Attorney authored the document, it seemed clear that he had included the statement as one of his arguments toward partition. It was his opinion. Or the statement originated from one or more of the plaintiffs as an excuse to file the lawsuit. From the perspective that the statement was about family matters as opposed to legal statements of fact, the topic could be debated and questioned.

Mr. Plaintiffs' Attorney's statement appeared to challenge the practicality of joint ownership by the plaintiffs and the defendants.

Defendants' Questions – Family

The statement, "For all practical purposes, it has become impossible for plaintiffs and defendants to jointly possess and enjoy the whole of the subject property" caught Rebecca's and William's attention as a first indication of debate. As Marta, Barbara, and Debra were well aware, owning and enjoying the property hadn't yet been tried.

Rebecca and William hoped that communication with their siblings could be restored, and the property saved. Still both periodically felt misgivings.

Their sisters' action seemed recklessly unreasonable and over-the-top. The bottom line was that the plaintiffs had completely refused face-to-face discussion about the property with their siblings prior to filing their lawsuit.

Rebecca and William wondered what their sisters hoped to gain. They knew that none of their sisters needed money. So was anger the issue? What had been the basis?

Yes, the five siblings had disagreed over the care of their aging parent and the pre-distribution of their parent's possessions. But in truth, the three sisters had kept the majority of their parent's possessions for themselves, in fact denying Rebecca and William their equal shares. Did they aspire to obtain more? Did they want the property for themselves, too?

Had there been any other conflict or disagreement in the family to warrant such an extreme action of filing a lawsuit? Rebecca and William considered every event that they could remember that had occurred over the last decade. They recalled that one or more of their sisters had initiated every dispute. But none of the disagreements seemed significant enough to initiate an action as intense and costly as a lawsuit, this time directly against Rebecca and William.

In their minds, Rebecca and William went back and forth considering every possible motive for their sisters' actions.

Filing a lawsuit? Rebecca and William agreed, "Unbelievable. The action is too extreme to comprehend."

Fact vs. Assumption

Separating fact from assumption became an ongoing challenge.

Using Mr. Plaintiffs' Attorney's statements as examples, some comments were 100% factual, such as those that stated the percentage of ownership of each of the five co-owners. Other statements that Mr. Plaintiffs' Attorney made implied factual content, however, were in truth assumptions on the part of that individual, some even in direct contradiction to assertions made by the defendants.

For example, Mr. Plaintiffs' Attorney repeatedly stated to the court and in legal documents that Rebecca and William had refused to sell thus requiring a partition. In fact, Rebecca and William had not refused to sell because their sisters had not presented them with an actual offer to buy.

Rebecca and William had expressed their love and interest in preserving the family property while not disputing the inevitable legal result of partition. As the lawsuit progressed, Rebecca and William repeated in court documents and verbally to the judge that they were willing to sell. Mr. Plaintiffs' Attorney continued to state that "defendants refuse to sell."

Rebecca and William wanted to explore every option toward settlement instead of continuing involvement in a costly legal action. They regarded the action of selling as only one of many options for preventing the continuing legal process.

The three plaintiffs had filed the lawsuit that implied that attempts toward a settlement had already occurred but had failed. In fact, Marta, Barbara, and Debra had skipped any face-to-face discussions with Rebecca and William and had instead jumped to the most extreme option available, filing their lawsuit.

Based on the fact that the partition lawsuit had already been filed and due to the absolute right of any of the co-owners, once an appraisal could be obtained, the matter could have legally concluded even before a pre-trial hearing took place through discussion with the plaintiffs' attorney. But no discussion took place.

Realistically, the property would be sold. So other, at the time unknown, factors affected the progress of the case.

The defendants formed additional questions:

What was the delay in finalizing the partition?

What did Mr. Plaintiffs' Attorney stand to gain by delaying the listing and the sale of the property?

Did the three plaintiffs expect that the defendants accept whatever the plaintiffs wanted without discussion or question allowing the plaintiffs complete and absolute control?

Defendants' Decision to Delay Hiring Attorney

Although it is perhaps common that defendants hire attorneys at this point for this particular legal action, Rebecca and William were reluctant to hire legal counsel before they knew their options. They were primarily concerned about the costs of hiring an attorney. Also, they didn't want to hire an attorney simply to battle back and forth without end with the plaintiffs' attorney. Neither of them had good experiences with the attorneys involved in their sisters' filing of their probate action against their parent. They were both acutely aware that they could innocently hire an individual that would work against them as had happened in their parent's case and at enormous cost. Additionally, for the most part, it seemed that the attorneys in that case overcharged and filed motion after motion for their purposes. So this time, Rebecca and William preferred to proceed cautiously.

Still, to be faced with a lawsuit is a very serious matter and potentially very costly with or without an attorney. So, Rebecca weighed the options that she was aware of at the time. Rebecca began to research different attorneys throughout the state where the property is located to learn what different lawyers charge and if they would be interested in representing William and her. She began by asking attorneys information about their fees. Several recommended that she contact lawyers close to the town in which the property is located. Rebecca continued to search. She was cognizant of the need to find an attorney with whom she felt comfortable, and whose charges were affordable.

Chapter III – The Answer

The Definition of an Answer to a Summons and Complaint

An *Answer* to a Summons and Complaint is a formal legal document in which the defendants respond to the plaintiffs' attorney and the plaintiffs. If the defendants fail to respond within the required length of time, the court may decide to award relief as the plaintiffs claim in the Summons and Complaint. The court can grant relief for some or all of the items listed in the Summons and Complaint.

Defendants Obtain Legal Advice

One of the attorneys that Rebecca had contacted advised her that William and Rebecca had to file separate Answers, a very important piece of good advice.

Whether it was the proper course of action to take or not, Rebecca found a template for an Answer specifically for the location of the property in the appropriate state. Next, Rebecca contacted an attorney to review the draft of her Answer. The attorney advised Rebecca to cooperate with Mr. Plaintiffs' Attorney to sell because in his opinion, the plaintiffs clearly weren't interested in discussion. Had they wanted discussion, the attorney explained, the plaintiffs would not have already filed the lawsuit. But that was an assumption on the lawyer's part since he hadn't spoken with any of the plaintiffs.

Rebecca considered the lawyer's advice. Rebecca along with William hadn't yet had a chance to settle. And they hadn't refused to sell because they hadn't been given a purchase agreement to review. They wanted the opportunity for a direct discussion with each of their three siblings without legal involvement. Unfortunately, unless their sisters agreed to drop their lawsuit, the legal process could not be reversed. It would continue to trial unless there was a settlement.

Additionally, there remained many contradictions and unanswered questions. Debra had stated in a voicemail to Rebecca over eight months before the transfer of the deed that Barbara had been in discussion with a potential buyer. But neither Debra nor Barbara had provided Rebecca or William with any solid information related to their alleged buyer either in the form of a purchase agreement or even general information about their exchanges.

Rebecca and William did not know if their sisters were bluffing or if they truly had a buyer. If they had a buyer, what was the reason for their secrecy? As equal owners, Rebecca and William had the right to information. But, for some reason, their sisters were deliberately withholding information from them.

Also, Debra claimed that Barbara and she had made multiple attempts to contact Rebecca and William, however stated that she had been unable to reach them. Both Rebecca and William recognized that the statement wasn't the truth.

Further, Rebecca felt that Debra had attempted to sucker her into providing information that the plaintiffs intended to later use against her. "Use of that tactic is probably one of the lowest forms of betrayal against family members", Rebecca pondered. "Why would she do that?"

Though the actions surely were pre-meditated, Rebecca and William didn't understand what their sisters hoped to gain. And why would their sisters, their own family members, use such subversive tactics against them?

Neither Marta nor Barbara had spoken their genuine feelings in their own words to either Rebecca or William.

For a nominal fee, the attorney made some suggestions to Rebecca to revise her Answer. He assured Rebecca that her Answer was sound and would be accepted by the court.

Defendants' Speculation of Outcomes

At the time, Rebecca and William, and very likely the plaintiffs, Mr. Plaintiffs' Attorney, and perhaps even the judge did not know if the sale of the property would be through an auction or a private sale. Rebecca was very concerned that the five co-owners could potentially lose most if not all of the equity of the property if an auction occurred.

Rebecca and William based their Answers on the primary factors that the plaintiffs had not provided sufficient information nor had communicated with the defendants so they could not respond with full knowledge. Each added additional topics to his or her Answer to offer suggestions that they hoped that the plaintiffs would accept and also to inform the judge about the background of the situation.

It seemed to Rebecca that the judge would take these matters into consideration. Most certainly, if the judge was without knowledge of the matters, then he could not consider the factors when making decisions.

Rebecca and William submitted their respective Answers separately.

Defendants' Answers

Rebecca's Answer to the court was dated July 11, 2012. William's Answer followed the next day.

Plaintiffs Refused Communication

The plaintiffs had neither initiated discussion for settlement options nor had the plaintiffs responded to any of Rebecca's communications. Both Rebecca and William stated that the plaintiffs had refused communication with them. Rebecca listed numerous examples of her attempted communications that included Rebecca's development of a password-protected website for use by the five siblings.

Defendants Agree to Sell
Defendant Requests that Plaintiffs Drop Lawsuit

Rebecca agreed to sell the property and expressed her suggestion to settle the situation outside of court. They knew that they both had no other choice but to agree to sell. However, they hoped that other options could be considered and discussed to end the lawsuit before they lost the property. Rebecca stated, "Defendant is agreeable to sell the property at market value and suggests that: 1. Plaintiffs agree to drop their lawsuit."

William also offered suggestions to prevent costly legal proceedings.

Both Rebecca and William stated in their respective answers that the plaintiffs and defendants had not yet tried joint ownership.

Management of the Property

Since no discussion had taken place on this topic, there was no plan in place to manage or protect the property. Rebecca and William requested that the plaintiffs and the defendants agree to manage the property without hiring outside parties to do so.

Appraisals

William stated in his Answer that the plaintiffs have not provided appraisals.

Receiver

William also stated that the plaintiffs have not clarified the need, role or estimates of the costs of hiring a Receiver.

William requested that the court rule against the appointment of a Receiver.

Rebecca agreed that a Receiver should not be appointed.

Defendants Request Same Financial Claims as Plaintiffs including Attorney Fees

Rebecca believed that to include claims for recovery of costs and attorney fees was standard and so included the sentence for that reason. As a layperson, Rebecca understood it to be a counter-claim to the plaintiffs' claims for the same relief. William requested the same claim.

Maintenance and Repairs

Rebecca and William had begun but had not completed maintenance and repair work on the property shortly before receiving the Summons and Complaint document. In response to Mr. Plaintiffs' Attorney's statement that pertained to leasing the property, William stated that the main building and garage are in need of repair and not suitable for lease or sale. To lease or sell the property, William believed that basic repair work needed to be completed before leasing the property to outside parties.

Insurance Premiums

Rebecca requested that the three plaintiffs reimburse William and her for each of their three shares of insurance premiums that Rebecca and William had paid. The plaintiffs appeared to oppose insuring the property.

Property Taxes

The plaintiffs had specifically withheld information from William and Rebecca about property taxes. To obtain tax information, Rebecca eventually contacted the appropriate tax assessors. Rebecca requested that each of the three plaintiffs pay their respective share of the property taxes.

Chapter IV – Pre-Trial

The Definition of a Pre-Trial

A *pre-trial conference* (Pre-Trial Conference, 2015) is "a meeting of the parties to an action and their attorneys held before the court prior to the commencement of actual courtroom proceedings . . . that may be conducted for several reasons: (1) expedite disposition of the case, (2) help the court establish managerial control over the case, (3) discourage wasteful pretrial activities, (4) improve the quality of the trial with thorough preparation, and (5) facilitate a settlement of the case."

The Hearing

The September 24, 2012 pre-trial proceeded rapidly and seemed to be over in a matter of minutes.

Mr. Plaintiffs' Attorney described that the case was between five siblings over an inherited-summer home that had been in the family for decades. He mentioned that the plaintiffs had a prospective buyer. And he stated that the defendants do not wish to sell.

The judge discussed the pre-trial document that Mr. Plaintiffs' Attorney had submitted to the court.

Judge's Direction

Obtain Appraisal

The judge directed Mr. Plaintiffs' Attorney to obtain an appraisal.

Participate in Mediation

The Honorable Mr. Impartial listened to Mr. Plaintiffs' Attorney and asked if the plaintiffs are open to mediation. Mr. Plaintiffs' Attorney stated, "Yes, plaintiffs are open to mediation." After another few minutes of legal comments by the judge, the Honorable Mr. Impartial turned to William and asked if he understood. Then he turned to Rebecca and asked her the same question.

Defendants' Perspectives

Rebecca noted that the Honorable Mr. Impartial appeared to direct his instructions only to Mr. Plaintiffs' Attorney. It was curious, Rebecca thought, that the judge had not told Rebecca and William to obtain their appraisal.

In a partition lawsuit, as opposed to other lawsuits where, for example, one party accuses the other of committing some civil or criminal offense, there has been no crime committed. Although Rebecca would learn that there exists a perception of wrongdoing on the part of the defendants simply by virtue of the fact that the plaintiffs filed a lawsuit, neither William nor she had committed an offense.

The plaintiffs placed Rebecca and William in the role of defendants in a surprise action. Since their sisters had not discussed anything with them, neither Rebecca nor William knew the basis of their complaint in terms of "it has become impossible for plaintiffs and defendants to jointly possess and enjoy the whole of the subject property." They did not know which sister was the primary initiator of the lawsuit or how the three had established their alliance.

At this time, neither Rebecca nor William had legal representation. As a result, neither knew the procedure that the court follows in a partition lawsuit.

Because neither Rebecca nor William knew what to expect, both felt a level of anxiety about the court procedure itself. Further, each felt distressed due to the impending loss of their property based on the basic amount of research each had done about partition up to this point. If they were to save their property, it was imperative that their sisters agree to discuss the situation with them and to arrive at some compromise. Otherwise, it was certain that the property would be lost.

Plaintiffs Not Present

Con: Apprehension - Possible Confrontation

Rebecca and William didn't know if any of their sisters would attend the hearing. They both felt apprehension about their sisters attending since neither Rebecca nor William wanted a confrontation. Their sisters' lawsuit was particularly aggressive, an action that came without warning and apparent basis.

Marta had used bullying tactics in the past toward Rebecca since childhood and particularly as an adult. Since neither Rebecca nor William had seen Marta in recent years, they didn't know if her behavioral pattern was unchanged. So both Rebecca and William believed that a risk existed that Marta was capable of seeming to provoke a quarrel and then rallying supporters by accusing Rebecca of initiating a confrontation. Marta had exhibited the behavior in the past on several occasions. Rebecca debated whether or not to inform the judge. Ultimately, she decided to trust that Marta had addressed her behavioral issues, although she remained concerned.

Pro: Learn Information

Both Rebecca and William thought it was unlikely that Marta would physically attend the hearing. Although Marta was more than financially able to afford travel, Rebecca and William believed that Marta would not view her attendance at the hearing as a priority. She had visited the property as a child, but not as much as an adult. Debra had rarely visited the property, although her daughter and her family had been recent guests. They believed that the person most likely to attend would be Barbara. Of all of the siblings, Barbara, and her family members had spent the most time at the property as guests of the five siblings' parent. Ideally, Rebecca and William thought that if all three of their sisters attended the hearing, maybe they could learn the truth behind their action and learn the motives of each.

No Discussion about the Defendants' Answers

There was no mention of either Rebecca's or William's Answers or acknowledgement that Rebecca and William had agreed to sell.

Pre-Trial Document Filed by Plaintiffs' Attorney

Mr. Plaintiffs' Attorney had filed a pre-trial document with the court in which he checked off or completed several legal points, one of which indicated that the plaintiffs were open to mediation. Since Rebecca and William are not attorneys, they did not know the purpose of the document that Mr. Plaintiffs' Attorney submitted. But, they understood that they needed to follow the process the best that they could.

Chapter V – Meeting with the Plaintiffs' Attorney and Obtaining Appraisals

Plaintiffs' Attorney's Questions Related to Property

Immediately following the pre-trial hearing, Rebecca and William met briefly with Mr. Plaintiffs' Attorney. None of their sisters had attended the hearing. Mr. Plaintiffs' Attorney responded to Rebecca and William that it was Marta who had filed the lawsuit. He appeared unwilling to answer other questions, instead responding by stating that he represented all three of Rebecca's and William's sisters.

Mr. Plaintiffs' Attorney asked Rebecca and William a series of questions. Among his questions and comments were:

"Where are the boundaries of the property? I'll need any surveys that have been done." Although Rebecca had a survey done years before for the purpose of investigating the possibility of building another residence for her parent on a separate lot, she did not know if the survey was still valid.

"We can sue the neighbors if they've built on the property." Neither Rebecca nor William had any intention to sue the neighbors. Rebecca didn't understand why Mr. Plaintiffs' Attorney made such a statement, a statement that seemed particularly aggressive without cause.

"I've sold many homes on this lake." Rebecca and William believed that Mr. Plaintiffs' Attorney was a lawyer and not a realtor. So, this comment seemed strange to both siblings.

"The house looks very rustic. Does it even have a toilet inside?" The main building is a lakefront log home with 1½ baths. Rebecca and William wondered the reason Mr. Plaintiffs' Attorney characterized the building as "rustic" in such a negative tone. It did not appear that he intended the term as a selling point.

Mr. Plaintiffs' Attorney stated, "Oh, mediation can be very expensive." Rebecca had asked Mr. Plaintiffs' Attorney when he would schedule the mediation. Only an hour before, Mr. Plaintiffs' Attorney had responded to the judge that the plaintiffs agreed to mediation. But now, Mr.

Plaintiffs' Attorney discouraged that mediation take place while not refusing to participate.

Defendants Request Information from Plaintiffs' Attorney about Plaintiffs' Buyer

Rebecca and William began to ask Mr. Plaintiffs' Attorney for information about their alleged buyer. Two days following the pre-trial hearing, Rebecca sent an email to Mr. Plaintiffs' Attorney asking him specifically for information about the buyer. Although he had indicated that the plaintiffs had a buyer, neither the plaintiffs nor Mr. Plaintiffs' attorney had given either Rebecca or William a purchase agreement document. Further, they had not given Rebecca and William any information whatsoever about their alleged buyer.

Defendants Send Email – Interest in Negotiating Buy-Out Price

On October 6, 2012, Rebecca sent an email to Mr. Plaintiffs' Attorney to advise him that William and she had sufficient means to buy out their sisters' three shares. They wanted to negotiate a buy-out price with the plaintiffs.

Defendants' Interpretations of Plaintiffs' Attorney's Questions and Lack of Response

By October 13, 2012, neither Rebecca nor William had received a response from Mr. Plaintiffs' Attorney to their questions. They did not know if Mr. Plaintiffs' Attorney's lack of response was the normal procedure or if it spoke to other issues. Specifically, Mr. Plaintiffs' Attorney had not answered their question about the plaintiffs' alleged buyer.

If the plaintiffs did not have a buyer, why had Rebecca's and William's sisters filed the lawsuit at that time? Now entering the fall and winter months, Rebecca and William anticipated a slow period when prospective buyers might not know about the property. They began to develop more questions about the legal process, however, had no means to have their questions answered.

Rebecca and William still did not have legal representation. Outside attorneys could only answer questions in very general terms. And Mr. Plaintiffs' Attorney seemed unwilling to answer Rebecca's and William's questions.

Rebecca and William believed that all topics (discussion of creative options, negotiation of a sale price, buy-out compromise, plan to preserve and rent the property, etc.) would be discussed and considered concurrently. They also assumed that a creative package could be developed using pieces from several alternatives.

They had not contested a sale or a partition. The defendants did not know how to make their position more clear.

Despite the fact that Rebecca and William each stated their willingness to sell, Mr. Plaintiffs' Attorney continued to maintain, "Defendants do not wish to sell" as if the defendants were contesting the partition.

Perhaps had the defendants had legal representation, their attorney could have responded. But at this time, the defendants preferred to represent themselves. They did not know how to reply and be heard by the court to Mr. Plaintiffs' Attorney's statements.

The Definition of Witness and Exhibit List

"An *exhibit list* is a listing of all documents or other tangible items (i.e., photographs, etc.) to be offered by a party for admission as evidence in support of that party's contentions . . . A *witness list* is a listing of all people a party intends to call to provide testimony in support of that party's contentions" (Exhibit and Witness Lists, 2015).

In both cases, unless documents and the names of witnesses appear on the witness and exhibit lists, the non-disclosed documents will not be admitted into evidence, and the unlisted individuals will not be permitted to testify.

Plaintiffs' Attorney's Witness and Exhibit List

Mr. Plaintiffs' Attorney listed the names of individuals ranging from tax assessors to appraisers, to realtors, brokers and yet named expert witnesses. The plaintiffs' attorney also listed a range of items to be used as possible evidence that included: public records, listing agreements, surveys, appraisals, insurance documents, and everything that the defendants had listed on their exhibit list.

Defendants' Witness and Exhibit List

Rebecca and William submitted a simplified list on October 21, 2012. Although their list was filed prior to the plaintiffs' attorney's filing of the document, it closely resembled the list that Mr. Plaintiffs' Attorney had submitted on October 23, 2012. It included the names of each of the individuals and documents listed by Mr. Plaintiffs' Attorney.

Defendants' Rationale for Filing Witness and Exhibit List

Rebecca and William understood that the attorney would use the lists in the event that a trial took place. Potentially extremely costly, and they believed, completely unnecessary since neither Rebecca nor William had refused to follow a partition or sale decision, the result of a trial seemed to be the worst outcome that could occur. Rebecca and William hoped that they could reach a settlement. But if the case did go to trial, Rebecca and William knew that if they did not file the Witness and Exhibit list, they would be unable to present any documentation and also could not call witnesses. The court procedure wouldn't have allowed the defendants to present anything. They wanted the opportunity to present their case and their documentation.

New Terms: Evidence, Discovery

The definition of *evidence* (Evidence, 2015) is: "every type of proof legally presented at trial (allowed by the judge) which is intended to convince the judge and jury of alleged facts material to the case. It can include oral testimony of witnesses, including experts on technical matters, documents, public records, objects, photographs and depositions (testimony under oath taken before trial). It also includes so-called "circumstantial evidence" which is intended to create belief by showing surrounding circumstances that logically lead to a conclusion of fact."

The definition of *discovery* (Discovery, 2015) is: "the entire efforts of a party to a lawsuit and his/her/its attorneys to obtain information before trial through demands for production of documents, depositions of parties and potential witnesses, written interrogatories (questions and answers written under oath), written requests for admissions of fact, examination of the scene and the petitions and motions employed to enforce discovery rights. The theory of broad rights of discovery is that all parties will go to trial with as much knowledge as possible and that neither party should be able to keep secrets from the other."

Defendants' Concerns to Date

Rebecca and William had numerous concerns at this point of the lawsuit. Among the most disconcerting was the lack of response from Mr. Plaintiffs' Attorney to their questions, particularly related to information about the plaintiffs' alleged buyer. Additionally, Rebecca and William were concerned about the potential cost of a trial. Both wanted to avoid a trial, however, did not know how to accomplish that.

The legal procedure seemed to be completely out of Rebecca's and William's control. Since neither had refused to sell the property, they didn't know what they were expected to do to bring the lawsuit to a close.

From their experiences with their late parent's probate situation and the procedures that were followed, they knew that the process could be lengthy. However, a probate case ends when the ward passes. This lawsuit was entirely different, instead involving real estate.

This case like the probate case against the siblings' parent was adversarial, intended as such when the plaintiffs filed the lawsuit as opposed to sitting down with their siblings to discuss options toward mutual agreed solutions. Related to the case were, of course, legal procedures, but this was also a family in distress.

Rebecca and William learned from their past experiences with their parent's probate case that their sisters had initiated that the adversarial process is not amicable. Instead the tactics that they observed being used most often were aimed at discrediting the other party, both in terms of discounting documents and facts, and also in the form of attacks in the forms of accusations against the other party, subtle and direct. In short, tactics used by some attorneys can be ugly, causing emotional pain and misery to family members who are already dealing with a major challenge in their lives, that of a lawsuit filed by their family members against them.

The adversarial process involves two opposing sides. It is simply the manner in which the American courts function. So, although, in partition lawsuits, neither party is usually at fault, accusations are often used to create a perception that one side has or will cause harm to the other. Since the definition of "harm" is not clearly explained in court documents, it is open to interpretation by the attorneys involved and also to the judge, who is an attorney. Therefore, attorneys might use the tactic of accusations to attempt to intimidate, discredit, or raise suspicion.

In many, if not most partition cases, a settlement is often reached between co-owners of properties with every option discussed long before the time when anyone even considers filing a lawsuit. A family member who plans to file a lawsuit will usually discuss with his or her other family members that he or she intends to file a lawsuit. Particularly in families, a discussion about every conceivable option, plus the knowledge of the other family member's intent to file a lawsuit can result in solutions and preservation of the family relationships. However, a red flag alert should be obvious if a family member files a lawsuit without warning and without having had any form of discussion whatsoever with the defendants.

The plaintiffs hired their attorney to act on the plaintiffs' behalf, and only on the plaintiffs' behalf.

Despite any outward acts of politeness on the part of the attorney toward the defendants, that fact remains as the reason the plaintiffs hired their attorney to initiate the lawsuit.

There are procedures such as discovery in which attorneys can formally require defendants to present information and documents to the plaintiffs' attorney in preparation for trial. However, in this partition case, there was little if any information that the defendants had, that the plaintiffs and the plaintiffs' attorney also did not have knowledge or access. Mr. Plaintiffs' Attorney routinely appeared to demand that Rebecca and William supply him with whatever information he wanted, however, did not respond to the defendants' requests for information. If Rebecca and William had legal representation at this point, perhaps the information would have been shared with their attorney. But at this point, Rebecca and William were simply trying to obtain as much information as possible to bring the matter to a close. Already they were faced with challenges that seemed unnecessary if the plaintiffs' goal was simply to sell the property.

Rebecca recognized that a double standard existed with the information given to the defendants. Mr. Plaintiffs' Attorney normally chose the aggressive tactic of expecting every piece of information, however offered little information to the defendants. He appeared to promise information that never materialized, such as the plaintiffs' alleged prospective buyer offer.

It seemed that the plaintiffs' attorney isn't required to provide the same or similar information to the defendants or can delay giving information to the defendants as long as it suits him.

Rebecca and William did not know about an apparent boundary that separates information that they obtained for their knowledge from information that Mr. Plaintiffs' Attorney wanted to use within the plaintiffs' lawsuit. They also were unaware that they had a supposed deadline to follow.

New Participants

Ms. Low Appraiser

Ms. High Appraiser

Defendants Have Appraisals Completed

Rebecca and William had two appraisals completed.
Rebecca had located the names of the appraisers by
researching appraisers in the area on the internet. Ms. High
Appraiser completed the first appraisal on November 5,
2012 shortly before dusk. Ms. Low Appraiser completed
the second appraisal the following day. Rebecca observed
the ease at which the appraisers completed their appraisals.
Neither appraiser gave Rebecca and William the results of
their respective appraisals immediately following their
visits to the property. It would take another week to
receive the results of one appraisal and longer to receive the
second appraisal results.

The Definition of Appraisal

The definition of a real estate *appraisal* (Appraisal,
2015) is: "a valuation of property by the estimate of an
authorized person. To be a valid appraisal, the authorized
person will have a designation of a regulatory body
governing the jurisdiction the appraiser operates within . . .
Appraisals are typically used either for taxation purposes or
to determine a possible selling price for the property in
question. The appraiser can use any number of valuation

methods to determine the appropriate value to assign, including the current market value of similar properties, quality of property and valuation models."

Defendants Receive Results of One Appraisal

About a week following the completion of the appraisals, Rebecca received the results of one from Ms. Low Appraiser.

Defendants' Purpose of Obtaining Appraisal

Without knowledge of the real-estate appraisal business, Rebecca and William did not know how appraisers determine the value of a property. So when they received the results of the first appraisal, they studied the document and looked at the photos of comparable properties in the area. Although the result seemed low, it was also Rebecca's and William's opinion that the amount that the appraiser determined for the value of the property was reasonable considering that repair work needed to be done on the property. As an independent appraiser, Ms. Low Appraiser did not stand to earn additional income if and when the property sold. She is a licensed appraiser, so her appraisal is valid. It would take another week or two to receive the results from the second appraiser, Ms. High Appraiser, an individual who works for a realtor in the area.

Rebecca's and William's purpose in obtaining the appraisals was that they wanted to know the approximate value of the property to determine what price they would offer and because of repairs that needed to be done so that anyone could comfortably live in the buildings. Once they received the results of Ms. Low Appraiser's appraisal, they decided to offer that as a starting point in negotiating a buy-out price with their sisters. Although they based their offer on Ms. Low Appraiser's appraisal result, they were not aware of the apparent requirement that a buyer's offer must be based on an appraisal figure.

Because Rebecca and William naively believed that the plaintiffs would negotiate, they did not necessarily intend Ms. Low Appraiser's appraisal as the final appraisal determination if negotiations with the plaintiffs failed. Rebecca and William were vaguely aware of a warning that the selling price and buy-out figure should be the same. However, in this partition case, negotiation had not yet occurred. So Rebecca and William innocently believed that their offer was reasonable. Both were unaware of any applicable partition rules.

At this point in the lawsuit, neither Rebecca nor William knew that Mr. Plaintiffs' Attorney intended to obtain the highest appraisal price as the final end appraisal figure in order to sell the property to a third party. Instead, both Rebecca and William believed that their sisters would either be willing to allow them to buy-out their three shares at the low appraisal amount due to repairs needed or would agree to negotiate a middle-ground price.

First Reason the Case Took Years to Complete

The first reason the case dragged on for over two years was the result of opposing interpretations such as those. Since Mr. Plaintiffs' Attorney intended to settle at only the highest appraisal price, the plaintiffs essentially had already refused to negotiate a compromise. Had Mr. Plaintiffs' Attorney informed the defendants of that fact rather than leading the defendants and the court to believe that mediation and negotiation were possible, the case could have been settled at this point.

Because of their love for the property, Rebecca and William wanted to attempt to save it by negotiating with their sisters. Their interest in negotiating didn't mean that they were contesting the partition or sale.

Mr. Plaintiffs' Attorney unfortunately used the defendants' sentimental attachment to the property to attempt to persuade the court that the defendants were refusing to sell, although both had stated otherwise in their Answers. Evidently, just by the fact that the defendants wanted to negotiate through discussion the option of saving the property, Mr. Plaintiffs' Attorney continued to claim that the defendants refuse to sell the property.

Plaintiffs' Purpose of Obtaining Appraisal

Mr. Plaintiffs' Attorney had two purposes of obtaining appraisals.

Ordered by Judge

The judge ordered Mr. Plaintiffs' Attorney to obtain an appraisal.

To Sell the Property

The legal purpose in obtaining an appraisal is to determine the value of the property to sell the property.

Plaintiffs' Appraisal Completed

Mr. Plaintiffs' Attorney had the plaintiffs' appraisal completed in late December 2012, three months after the judge ordered him to obtain an appraisal, and eight months after the plaintiffs filed their lawsuit.

Chapter VI – Mediation

Why Choose Mediation?

Attorney Robert I. Levy (2014) explained that "the only participants in the partition action that truly benefit from the partition action are the attorneys . . . Lawsuits are expensive and if it is possible to avoid a partition action and resolve the dispute before it escalates to a lawsuit, it is in everybody's interest to do so because of the costs associated with a partition action." The alternative that Mr. Levy suggested is mediation.

Sher (2010) described an example of mediation: "Mediation increasingly occurs in the context of family trust disputes. Consider four siblings, all beneficiaries under their deceased parents' trust, which includes the former family home and another property currently leased to one of the siblings. Three accuse the eldest sibling, as successor trustee following the death of the surviving parent of mismanagement, self-dealing, commingling her funds with trust funds and making gifts to non-beneficiaries. They demand sale of the real property and an accounting and seek to "surcharge" their sister's interest with not only the alleged losses but also attorney's fees and costs of prosecuting the partition/accounting action. The sibling who is renting from the trust enjoys a below-market rent and wants to continue as a tenant. The disputants risk spending all of their time, energy, and the trust estate in litigation."

In December of 2009, Folberg described his experiences with mediating partition disputes: "Of all of the cases I have mediated over the past 30 years, the most challenging and rewarding disputes have been those between family members over family property, estates, trusts, and businesses. Brothers and sisters may fight over partnership property, but they are really sorting out old issues of sibling rivalry and dominance. Once a patriarch or matriarch of a family has given up control or passed away, adult children are often left in a position of ambiguity or, worse, contrary beliefs about their rightful role. Disputes surface that are usually less about malevolence than about conflicting feelings, misunderstandings of intent, divergent expectations, and resistance to change or unspoken fears."

The benefits of mediation, either direct mediation in which face-to-face negotiation occurs, or assisted mediation where a mediator facilitates the negotiation process (Arbitration and Mediation, 2015) as opposed to litigation are: "Costs to both plaintiffs and defendants are kept low, the parties retain control of the outcome of the case, relationships between the parties can usually be preserved and it is a less hostile, less confrontational format for resolving disputes" (Arbitration and Mediation, 2015). Besides the potentially extreme financial cost of litigation, there is a risk in litigating because the outcome is uncertain due to the fact that judges can rule either way or "make mistakes" (Levy, 2014).

The article "Arbitration and Mediation" (Arbitration and Mediation, 2015) explained the issues with litigation in greater detail: "Courtrooms are very formal, intimidating places . . , the evidence that the court can consider is limited . . , attorneys in formal trials who are experts in procedure and evidence rules charge by the hour . . , trials can last weeks, months or even years . . , and it is emotionally draining and unpredictable."

Normally done before a plaintiff files a lawsuit, mediation can prevent many problems later and can lead instead to preserved relationships among family members and a Win-Win resolution. It is better late than never to at least attempt mediation if the lawsuit has already been filed. Discussions between the plaintiffs' attorney and the defendants can take place at any time.

But month after month, discussions did not occur in Rebecca's and William's family's case.

The Definitions of Mediation and Arbitration

Mediation differs from arbitration in that, "*arbitration is essentially a private trial*" (Levy, 2014), or "a quicker, lighter version of a trial where a third party called an arbitrator makes a decision about the case" (Arbitration and Mediation, 2015), whereas *mediation* is a "process where the parties and their attorneys get together with a neutral third party, usually a retired judge or an attorney, and collectively attempt to resolve or settle their dispute" (Levy, 2014).

Recommended Questions to Ask at a Mediation

According to Malcolm Sher (2010), "prior to initiating the partition action, counsel should ask the clients what their goals are." In this way, settlement terms might be determined more easily. For use during mediation, Mr.

Sher recommended that mediators ask a series of questions that include: "Does one party need money quickly? Can the sale take advantage of market conditions? Will the sale be at an auction or through a private contract? Can the market value of the property be agreed upon, at least for listing purposes? Will the parties accept a Comparative Market Analysis by an experienced broker or is a formal appraisal absolutely essential? If there is no acceptable offer within an agreed-upon timeframe, will the parties defer to the listing broker to decide the timing and size of price reductions? What needs to be done to ready the property for sale and will the parties agree to split the cost?"

Although Mr. Sher's example of mediation involves discussion that appears limited to the sale of a property, additional questions related to options for preserving the property can be asked. What creative options are available?

Negotiating Techniques

Mediation commonly entails the use of negotiating techniques. But how or even if attorneys and others use those techniques can differ greatly depending on the interpretation of the value of negotiation.

It is important that all of the participants are transparent about the topics to be discussed. If the plaintiffs are concerned only that the defendants pay their attorney fees while the defendants are focused instead on preventing further legal action, the mediation won't be successful if attention isn't given to all areas of focus. Recognition of the perspectives of the plaintiffs and the defendants is needed for genuine success to occur.

Therefore, if both parties submit an agenda of topics prior to mediating, the action may help in defining the mediation discussion topics and preventing future delays. The key to achieving a successful mediation is to work toward Win-Win solutions in which all parties feel respected and heard with concessions made toward success for each co-owner. While there is no guarantee that the plaintiffs will agree to submit a list of proposed discussion topics or that every topic will be discussed, the defendants will learn and be able to measure how cooperative the plaintiffs' attorney will be based on his willingness to be transparent.

However, in a partition lawsuit, the defendants' preferences are unfortunately usually viewed as irrelevant. Once a lawsuit has been filed, the property will be sold regardless. Arriving at an agreement is really the only way to save a property once a lawsuit has been filed. The topic of saving the property needs to be added to the agenda for discussion to occur. The catch is if the plaintiffs agree to save the property and either drop the lawsuit or consider creative solutions that satisfy every co-owner. It is a long shot, but one worth pursuing if the plaintiffs are open to that topic of discussion. There are many scenarios that can result depending on the plaintiffs' level of cooperation.

Kristi Hedges (Dec, 2013) offered six negotiation techniques in her article, "Six Surprising Negotiation Tactics That Get You the Best Deal: "1. Share information. If we want to be trusted, we must first offer it. 2. Rank order your priorities. Grant's research shows that you are able to achieve better outcomes by ranking and leaving all the issues on the table and being transparent about it. 3. Go in knowing your target price and your walkaway terms. Galinsky calls your walkaway price (or terms) your reservation price. Your target price is what you're hoping for. 4. Make the first offer. Grant and Galinsky both agree that the research is clear on this point: people who make first offers get better terms that are closer to their target price. The reason is the psychological principle of anchoring. Whatever the first number is on the table, both parties begin to work around it. It sets the stage. 5. Don't counter too low. Your counter should be based on the same information you would have used if you'd made the first offer, Galinsky says. 6. Counter offers make both parties more satisfied. By going back and forth and asking for concessions, you can ensure that you got the best deal and increase your partner's (the other parties') satisfaction as well."

New Participants

Ms. Mediator

Mr. Mediator

Mediation Hearing

The mediation hearing that Rebecca arranged and scheduled took place on November 29, 2012. Rebecca located the mediation team through the internet. The cost of this mediation was very affordable at only $100.

Rebecca found other pricings of mediation to be up to
$2000 per day.

Plaintiffs Technically Had Already Refused Mediation

The Honorable Mr. Impartial ordered mediation at the
Pre-Trial Hearing, which is a usual procedure in a lawsuit
(Arbitration and Mediation, 2015). But Mr. Plaintiffs'
Attorney had not begun to arrange or schedule mediation to
occur. Since the plaintiffs filed their lawsuit without
discussion, they essentially had already refused mediation.
The plaintiffs had not discussed anything about the details
of a sale with the defendants. Whatever their plan, the
plaintiffs appeared to desire absolute control without input
from the defendants, equal co-owners of the property.

Plaintiffs Refuse to Attend

Rebecca and William were aware that none of the
plaintiffs intended to attend the mediation. A few days
earlier, they had each received a copy of a letter that Mr.
Plaintiffs' Attorney had mailed to the court clerk that his
clients would not be attending the meeting. Mr. Plaintiffs'
Attorney explained that "it is impossible for our client to
appear in person due to the holiday weekend, and the

extraordinary expense for travel . . . That his client was not trying to avoid active participation . . . That his client would appear if the matter went to trial . . . And that his client would be available via telephone." Mr. Plaintiffs' Attorney further stated, "We believe that we are extremely close to a settlement."

Since the plaintiffs refused to attend, there could be no direct discussion with the defendants. This mediation emphasized an aggressive and adversarial legal approach by the plaintiffs as opposed to an amicable discussion between blood relatives.

Plaintiffs Agreed to Mediation Only for Appearances

Since none of the plaintiffs agreed to be physically present at the mediation nor did any of them connect by telephone to the actual meeting, it seemed that they or Mr. Plaintiffs' Attorney agreed to mediation only for appearances sake. While mediation is not a process that could prevent the ultimate sale of the property, acceptance of mediation implied to the defendants that the plaintiffs were willing to negotiate.

Plaintiffs' Refusal to Negotiate

Mr. Plaintiffs' Attorney's statement that "we believe that we are extremely close to settlement" made no sense to Rebecca and William since Mr. Plaintiffs' Attorney had not discussed any settlement options at all with either of them. They had not spoken on the telephone, and the only meeting that had taken place had been when Rebecca and William had first met Mr. Plaintiffs' Attorney after the pre-trial hearing in September 2012. In fact, Mr. Plaintiffs' Attorney had consistently ignored each and every email that Rebecca sent asking him to respond to their questions. He had not yet obtained an appraisal. Negotiation about a buy-out hadn't begun. And he had not provided information about the plaintiffs' alleged buyer.

Plaintiffs' Attorney Requests

During the mediation, Mr. Plaintiffs' Attorney primarily focused on two terms of his interpretation of settlement. He wanted Rebecca and William to agree to each pay 1/5 of his attorney fees, and he expected each of them to supply the plaintiffs' attorney with their complete financial records.

Plaintiffs' Attorney Rejects Ms. Low Appraiser's Appraisal

Since Rebecca and William had received the results of Ms. Low Appraiser's appraisal prior to the mediation, they presented that document to Mr. Plaintiffs' Attorney and the mediators. Mr. Plaintiffs' Attorney immediately disagreed with the appraisal result of $161,000, and declared that he would reject it. He stated that he expected an appraisal of the property to be $139,000 more than Ms. Low Appraiser's appraisal at $300,000. Neither Rebecca nor William argued the point with Mr. Plaintiffs' Attorney. They simply presented the information to Mr. Plaintiffs' Attorney. There was no discussion pertaining to a Competitive Market Analysis of the property.

Mediators' Recommendations to Defendant

The mediators offered several recommendations to Rebecca. First, the mediators suggested that Rebecca file a motion with the court to accept Ms. Low Appraiser's appraisal. Second, the mediators encouraged Rebecca and William to agree to pay part of Mr. Plaintiffs' Attorney's his attorney fees since "one can never know what a judge will decide." Third, the mediators encouraged the defendants to accept statements made in general rather than specific terms.

Rebecca and William made note of the fact that the mediators had not directed similar cautions to Mr. Plaintiffs' Attorney regarding decisions that a judge could make.

When Rebecca set up the mediation, the coordinator stated that she would attempt to encourage at least one of the plaintiffs to be present. So, Rebecca asked, "How can the mediation proceed when the three plaintiffs aren't present and active participants?" One of the mediators answered, "The plaintiffs might give conflicting statements."

The problem was that without direct discussion with their siblings, Rebecca and William would not learn the true reasons behind their siblings' actions. They both knew that there was more to their sisters' action than simply desiring the sale of the property.

Rebecca realized that her general expectation of what mediation entailed was faulty. It wasn't about compromise, mutual conversation, or even discussion about a sale. This mediation involved Mr. Plaintiffs' Attorney dictating demands to the defendants.

Plaintiffs' Terms from Defendants' Perspective

Although it was obvious that Mr. Plaintiffs' Attorney wanted Rebecca and William to agree to pay part of his attorney fees, it wasn't clear if that would be a deal breaker if Rebecca and William refused to agree to those terms. Additionally, there were other factors that related to agreeing or not agreeing to payment of part of Mr. Plaintiffs' Attorney's fees. Exactly what were Mr. Plaintiffs' Attorney's charges? He hadn't said. Did agreement to pay mean that the defendants would be giving up their right to obtain legal counsel? Did agreement to pay mean that the defendants were also agreeing to allow the plaintiffs complete control and decision making regarding the property? There had been no discussion about those three matters. Without legal counsel, Rebecca believed that to agree to vague terms was not in the best interest of either of the defendants.

To Rebecca and William, Mr. Plaintiffs' Attorney's stated conditions – particularly that the defendants supply him with their financial records - were so extreme that few would ever accept them.

Further, Rebecca and William didn't know Mr. Plaintiffs' Attorney's interpretation of exactly what specific conditions and terms a settlement entailed in his view. Rebecca asked the specific question numerous times again without a response from Mr. Plaintiffs' Attorney. Couldn't the plaintiffs be specific and list their terms one by one?

Essentially Rebecca and William believed that Mr. Plaintiffs' Attorney was not transparent in communicating information to them. What information was he hiding?

Plaintiffs Hadn't Considered Odds of Winning, Bottom Line, Options or Time Spent Negotiating

It was clear to Rebecca and William that the plaintiffs hadn't considered: "the odds of winning a lawsuit, their bottom line, different options for settlement, or the amount of time spent on negotiating" (Arbitration and Mediation, 2015). The plaintiffs had simply filed the lawsuit as their first choice rather than the last option without consideration of the consequences. So convinced that they would win, they were determined to have their way no matter what.

But how could they be declared the winners when the end result of a partition lawsuit is always sale of the property unless a settlement is reached?

Defendants Lack Legal Knowledge

Since Rebecca and William offered Ms. Low Appraiser's appraisal document in their perspective as a starting point in negotiation, they initially did not know how to respond to Mr. Plaintiffs' Attorney's statement that he would reject the appraisal. At the time, Mr. Plaintiffs' Attorney had not had his appraisal completed. He only stated, "We expect the appraisal to come back at $300,000."

Neither Rebecca nor William knew if the filing of motions with the court was required for the court to accept appraisals. If the court required the filing of motions for every legal process, Rebecca and William saw potential court costs mounting. They both wanted an amicable settlement, but saw that the adversarial nature of the contest was simply increasing instead despite their best intents. Additionally, they recognized that the only way to settle was to continue to work through the process to learn what options remained available to them to protect their rights as equal owners.

Defendants' Current Views

Neither Rebecca nor William had refused to sell. And neither had refused the results of the plaintiffs' attorney's appraisal that he had not obtained yet. At the time of the mediation, Rebecca and William believed that the plaintiffs might discuss a compromise. Since they knew that a buy-out was one option that they could pursue, they attempted that as a first step toward a settlement.

Creative Options Not Discussed

Had the mediation occurred prior to the plaintiffs' filing of their lawsuit, the focus might have included discussion about listing the property, the sale of the property either by an auction or by listing the property, maintenance of the property, and certainly creative options such as renting the property for long-term use toward profit for each of the co-owners. Since no discussion of any of those areas took place, there was no opportunity for compromise with the plaintiffs. The mediation instead took a different path apparently as directed by Mr. Plaintiffs' Attorney.

Plaintiffs' Vague Focus

It appeared long after the fact that Mr. Plaintiffs' Attorney was focused only on selling the property without consideration of how the sale would occur. The defendants had researched that the usual legal options in a partition case are buy-out, sale by listing, and sale by auction. But there had been no discussion with Mr. Plaintiffs' Attorney about each of those options. So, the defendants could only guess what option the plaintiffs were considering in their lawsuit.

The plaintiffs still had not responded to Rebecca's and William's request for information about their alleged buyer. There was no discussion about listing the property that apparently was delayed by the time it took to obtain the appraisals. Aside from informing each other about the appraisal results, no discussion occurred between the plaintiffs and the defendants about the appraisals' details.

Second Reason the Case Took Years to Complete

The time that it took for Mr. Plaintiffs' Attorney to collect and debate the appraisal findings was the second reason for the lengthy over-two-year process to complete.

Plaintiffs Not Interested in Preserving Relations

Rebecca and William gradually understood that the plaintiffs likely were not interested in discussion of different remedies to "keep good relations" (Arbitration and Mediation, 2015). The exchange of alternative options other than money could have been discussed to preserve good relations if not the property. The plaintiffs' absence from the mediation indicated that the preservation of family relationships was not their priority.

Defendants' Formal Offer to Buy-Out Plaintiffs

A few days after the mediation, Rebecca and William submitted a formal offer to buy-out their sisters' three shares based on Ms. Low Appraiser's appraisal and adjusted to the three shares. Besides hoping to save the property, Rebecca and William also believed that the plaintiffs would prefer to sell the property to their siblings at the appraisal price that appeared to consider the needed repairs. They also erroneously thought that their offer might prevent a sale by an auction since their offer was higher than that which an auction would presumably bring.

They did not realize that the judge would likely have followed a procedural rule to order an auction, and dismissed their offer. At best, Rebecca and William thought that the plaintiffs would agree to their offer. At worst, they believed that it was simply a starting point for settlement and to conserve costs for all five co-owners.

Chapter VII – Hearing; Plaintiffs' Surprise Offer to Settle

Pre-Hearing Surprise Offer to Settle

The day before the second hearing was scheduled to take place in late January 2013, Mr. Plaintiffs' Attorney contacted William to advise him that the plaintiffs had established a counter-offer.

Mr. Plaintiffs' Attorney had offered that the defendants buy-out their three shares at the Comparative Market Analysis figure of $235,000. He didn't discuss any other terms at the time.

Literally minutes prior to the start of the hearing Mr. Plaintiffs' Attorney advised Rebecca that if the defendants agreed to accept the plaintiffs' counter-offer, the defendants would also have to pay all of the property taxes including the plaintiffs' shares. Payment of the taxes would have brought the cost to the defendants to approximately $250,000, the amount of Ms. High Appraiser's appraisal.

As yet, Mr. Plaintiffs' Attorney had not given the defendants the results of Mr. Plaintiffs' Attorney's Appraiser's appraisal.

Although the plaintiffs had agreed during the mediation to reimburse Rebecca and William for payments of property taxes that the two of them had made, the three plaintiffs had not paid any taxes to date nor had they given Rebecca and William any money in reimbursement.

Purpose of Hearing

The apparent purpose of the second hearing was to discuss if a settlement had occurred.

Hearing

Rebecca and William described the history and their love for the property to the judge. He appeared unaffected. To the court, the topic seemed irrelevant.

Rebecca and William had not expected that the judge, The Honorable Mr. Impartial would discuss the idea of a demolition of the property buildings. Since the main reason why Rebecca and William would buy-out their sisters was related to the memories that they had with family in the particularly warm environment of the knotty-pine-walled main residence, to demolish the buildings would terminate their interest in the property.

Rebecca and William presented that realtors publish information about buildings within their appraisals. As such, the building values are part of the appraisal price. Neither Rebecca nor William refused the idea of demolition. However, Rebecca wondered why the subject of demolition came up. Clearly Mr. Plaintiffs' Attorney had proposed the idea to the judge, perhaps using his negative characterization of the buildings. The plaintiffs had not discussed the topic of a demolition with either Rebecca or William previously.

Rebecca and William wondered about Mr. Plaintiffs' Attorney's logic. They were aware of another lakefront property several miles north of their property that had been on the market for years. It was an empty lot. Was it wise to demolish buildings at the expense of the current owners? If a new buyer materialized, he would determine whether to keep or demolish the buildings anyway. Further, as long as the lawsuit continued, the five co-owners could be paying the taxes on an empty lot that none could use if the buildings were demolished. Had the plaintiffs thought this through?

The judge asked the defendants if they agreed to sell the property. First Rebecca responded, "Yes, I agree to sell the property." Then, William stated, "Yes, I agree to sell the property." Neither Rebecca nor William argued against selling or partition of the property.

Judge Asks Plaintiffs' Attorney about Buyer's Offer

The judge next asked Mr. Plaintiffs' Attorney about their alleged buyer's offer. Mr. Plaintiffs' Attorney responded, "I will have to check on that."

The Honorable Mr. Impartial stared at Mr. Plaintiffs' Attorney for what seemed like several minutes. There was no other response from Mr. Plaintiffs' Attorney in answer to the judge's question.

The Honorable Mr. Impartial's Statement: "It's as if you did the appraisal yourself."

The judge touched on the subject of Ms. Low Appraiser's appraisal. He commented that he believed that the appraisal was low. The judge didn't clarify if he would never accept the appraisal amount as an offer or accept it as an alternative to selling the property at auction. Nor did the judge state that he was rejecting the appraisal. However,

The Honorable Mr. Impartial implied suspicion. "It's as if you did the appraisal yourself."

Rebecca silently listened to the judge's comments wondering why the judge seemed so suspicious. Had the plaintiffs' attorney raised the topic without the defendants' knowledge? In the small town where the property is located, surely all of the judges know each and every appraiser. Additionally, Ms. Low Appraiser is a licensed appraiser. Ms. Low Appraiser had submitted a formal document to Rebecca that included information about which Rebecca is not an expert.

Rebecca and William had presented that formal document to Mr. Plaintiffs' Attorney at the mediation. Mr. Plaintiffs' Attorney had stated during the mediation that he would reject Ms. Low Appraiser's appraisal. So, had Mr. Plaintiffs' Attorney attempted to persuade the judge by himself accusing Rebecca? It seemed likely and also probable.

But, Rebecca did not understand why the judge was implying suspicion of Rebecca's actions and was also essentially questioning Ms. Low Appraiser's professional evaluation.

Although she felt it grossly unfair to be accused, Rebecca remained silent simply shaking her head at the ludicrous idea that she would have attempted to submit a do-it-yourself appraisal. Formal appraisals are completed by licensed individuals. She wondered if there was a parallel to the fact that neither William nor she had legal representation.

Rebecca realized that she was at a disadvantage since she was without legal representation. But Rebecca had done nothing to warrant being accused except to obtain an appraisal. Had she crossed a line? Was accusing defendants common in court cases? Rebecca didn't know. She believed that the accusation, like the idea to demolish the buildings on the property were both Mr. Plaintiffs' Attorney's tactics as part of the adversarial process. To attempt to discredit Rebecca and Ms. Low Appraiser appeared to be one of the several motives.

Judge Recommends Appointment of a Third Appraiser

The judge next recommended the appointment of a third appraiser. He stated that he would accept three choices of appraisers from the plaintiffs and three choices of appraisers from the defendants. Then from those six suggestions, the judge would choose one appraiser who would perform the third appraisal.

New Participants

Mr. Third Appraiser

Mr. Plaintiffs' Attorney's Appraiser

Purpose of Third Appraiser – Defendants' Perspective

Based on The Honorable Mr. Impartial's statements, Rebecca and William concluded that it was the judge's intent that the plaintiffs with the two defendants would negotiate a price between the low and high appraisals.

At the time that the judge recommended the appointment of a third appraiser, Rebecca and William believed that it was mutually understood that Ms. Low Appraiser's appraisal would be used as the low figure.

They did not understand that the low appraisal figure used could change.

The judge then encouraged Rebecca and William that they could feel free to discuss their three choices with Mr. Plaintiffs' Attorney. Unfortunately, Rebecca and William did not feel confident that Mr. Plaintiffs' Attorney would extend them the same courtesy.

Purpose of Third Appraiser – Plaintiffs' Attorney's Perspective

Mr. Plaintiffs' Attorney stated that he agreed to the appointment of the third appraiser. He was physically present when the judge recommended that negotiations could take place to find a middle ground. So, it appeared that he understood that the purpose of appointing the third appraiser was that negotiation would follow.

Defendants' Perspective to Date

At this point in the lawsuit, Rebecca and William continued to doubt that the plaintiffs had a buyer. And due to the fact that Mr. Plaintiffs' Attorney had not responded to Rebecca's and William's multiple attempts to ask questions of him, they also doubted that Mr. Plaintiffs'

Attorney would be forthcoming with any information at all.
It seemed unlikely to Rebecca and William that Mr.
Plaintiffs' Attorney would share his three choices of
appraisers with them.

Rebecca and William also discussed that Mr. Plaintiffs'
Attorney had waited until the day before the hearing was
scheduled to present the plaintiffs' counter-offer to them.
He had not given either Rebecca or William any
documentation about the Competitive Market Analysis
until a few minutes before the hearing started, and even
then he simply waved it in front of Rebecca's eyes.
Therefore, Rebecca and William had no time at all to
review or discuss the documents.

If the expectation was that Rebecca and William make
a snap decision, they didn't know. It was clear to both
Rebecca and William that Mr. Plaintiffs' Attorney desired
to avoid any discussion that involved the give and take of
ideas and options for a settlement.

Plaintiffs' Attorney: "It's not my job to encourage the plaintiffs to communicate with you."

As the hearing ended, Rebecca turned to Mr. Plaintiffs' Attorney and asked him why he hadn't encouraged the three plaintiffs to communicate directly with the defendants. After all, so much time and aggravation could have been saved had each of the plaintiffs simply directly expressed their wishes to their siblings. With discussion, many options could have already been discussed. And family relationships could have been renewed rather than broken due to this adversarial contest.

Mr. Plaintiffs' Attorney turned to Rebecca and stated brusquely, "It's not my job to encourage my clients to communicate with you."

Third Reason the Case Took Years to Complete

A third reason the case took years to complete came as a result of the plaintiffs' refusal to communicate with the defendants, and Mr. Plaintiffs' Attorney's refusal to encourage each of the three plaintiffs to communicate directly with the two defendants.

Chapter VIII – Hearing; Naming an Independent Appraiser

Defendants Submit Three Appraiser Names to Judge

A couple of weeks following the January 2013 hearing, Rebecca and William discussed and agreed to three independent appraiser names. They submitted the three names to the judge. A short time later, they each received a letter from the court that the judge had selected the third appraiser, Mr. Third Appraiser from the lists that the defendants and Mr. Plaintiffs' Attorney submitted.

Purpose of Hearing

The next hearing took place on April 2, 2013. As with the first hearing, this meeting was held in a large courtroom with The Honorable Mr. Impartial presiding. Although Mr. Plaintiffs' Attorney physically attended the two previous hearings, this time he connected by teleconference call.

The Honorable Mr. Impartial asked Rebecca and William to approach his desk. Both defendants stood at the judge's desk for the duration of the hearing.

The purpose of the hearing appeared to be to update the judge on the third appraisal.

Plaintiffs' Attorney Complains – Accuses Defendants of Withholding Ms. High Appraiser's Appraisal

The hearing began with Mr. Plaintiffs' Attorney directly accusing the defendants of withholding Ms. High Appraiser's appraisal from him. Rebecca and William hadn't expected that Ms. High Appraiser's appraisal would become an issue.

The two defendants had researched that appraisals are interpretations of the value of a property. It made sense that the different appraisers could have different opinions of the value of the property. Further, it seemed fair to Rebecca and William that a compromise would involve finding the middle ground between the low and high appraisals. They began to realize that Mr. Plaintiffs' Attorney, in contrast, focused on the number of appraisals with similar results. The larger the number of appraisals that he could obtain at the same result, the more vigorously he would argue that was the only valid appraisal amount.

Since the January 2012 hearing, Mr. Plaintiffs' Attorney had given the result of Mr. Plaintiff's Attorney's Appraiser to Rebecca and William. The result was $258,000, $8,000 higher than Ms. High Appraiser's appraisal.

Mr. Plaintiffs' Attorney asked the judge, "Is there a need for another appraisal?"

The Honorable Mr. Impartial decided the third appraisal was still warranted, asked if it had been completed, and what was the result. Rebecca and William shook their heads to indicate that they had no knowledge that Mr. Plaintiffs' Attorney had initiated it. They assumed that Mr. Plaintiffs' Attorney was making the arrangements to have the appraisal done. Mr. Plaintiffs' Attorney also indicated that the appraisal had not been completed.

The Honorable Mr. Impartial seemed exasperated that the appraisal had not been finished. Mr. Plaintiffs' Attorney stated, "I spoke to the appraiser today. It will be done soon."

Defendant's Conversation with Third Appraiser

Following the hearing, Rebecca and William telephoned Mr. Third Appraiser to see if they could expedite the process.

Mr. Third Appraiser told Rebecca that he had not spoken to Mr. Plaintiffs' Attorney and rather that Mr. Plaintiffs' Attorney had left him a voicemail only that morning. As Rebecca briefly explained the situation to the appraiser, it seemed that he was reluctant to speak with her because the appraisal was court ordered. The appraiser assured her, however, that he would add the appraisal to his schedule, but because he was very busy that it might take weeks to complete.

Rebecca sent a letter to the court in which she requested that the court formally approve that the third appraisal be completed with a letter sent to the third appraiser. As long as the third appraisal was not completed, Rebecca and William believed, negotiation could not take place with the plaintiffs.

Defendant's Perspective

A major challenge to Rebecca and William at this point in the lawsuit was still that Mr. Plaintiffs' Attorney was only minimally communicating with the defendants. Additionally, although the court had directed the appointment of a third appraiser, there appeared to be no plan as to who would arrange the third appraisal. Perhaps Mr. Plaintiffs' Attorney assumed that a court representative would arrange for the appraisal, or he was simply delaying initiating the process himself. In any event, it hadn't as yet been completed.

It seemed that Mr. Plaintiffs' Attorney preferred to add to the adversarial approach that the plaintiffs had initiated and accuse the defendants rather than simply communicate with them.

Rebecca and William realized that Mr. Plaintiffs' Attorney intended to ignore any appraisals except the highest. Unfortunately, however, the plaintiffs' attorney at the same time was implying that the plaintiffs were willing to negotiate with Rebecca and William to find a mutually acceptable common price. It didn't occur to Rebecca and William that Mr. Plaintiffs' Attorney apparently limited his range of negotiation to $3,000 or less. In truth, he and the plaintiffs were unwilling to budge significantly.

Another issue that came up at this time was if costs would be split 50/50 between the plaintiffs and the defendants or 60/40 between the three plaintiffs and the two defendants. Rebecca and William asserted that the plaintiffs should not receive a discount no matter how small the cost. Although the mediation cost of $100 was split equally in half between the two sides, Rebecca and William hoped that all other costs would be the equal responsibility of each of the five co-owners.

According to Mr. Third Appraiser, Mr. Plaintiffs' Attorney had led him to believe that the costs for his appraisal would be split 50/50.

Chapter IX – Hearing; Independent Appraisal Not Completed

Purpose of Hearing

The fourth hearing took place on May 20, 2013, with the assumed purpose of updating the judge on the progress to date.

Mr. Plaintiffs' Attorney and William both connected by teleconference call to this hearing. Ms. Low Appraiser accompanied Rebecca to the hearing. Rebecca and William had not subpoenaed Ms. Low Appraiser. Rather, Ms. Low Appraiser volunteered to attend the hearing.

This hearing took place in the chambers of The Honorable Mr. Impartial as had the January 2013 hearing.

Topics Discussed

The hearing took only about fifteen minutes to complete. The third appraisal still had not been completed.

In a new development, Mr. Plaintiffs' Attorney suggested that the appraisers meet as a group.

The judge stressed that creative options can be used to settle.

Defendants' Perspective

Since Ms. Low Appraiser was in attendance at this hearing, Rebecca and William believed that the appraiser would be included in the meeting that Mr. Plaintiffs' Attorney proposed take place between the appraisers.

Rebecca and William were of the understanding that the appraisers would meet, discuss their respective appraisals and compromise on a middle ground value of the property. The Honorable Mr. Impartial had implied that course of action would take place.

The defendants further naively believed that the three appraisers would meet with the defendants informally to discuss their findings before also presenting their results informally to The Honorable Mr. Impartial. Rebecca and William were completely unaware that Mr. Plaintiffs' Attorney was perhaps contemplating using a plan against the defendants. He had stated after all that the matter could be settled amicably.

Such an approach to simply share the information would have been amicable. Instead, Mr. Plaintiffs' Attorney chose to continue the adversarial approach by implying that Rebecca and William had and would contest the higher appraisals. Neither Rebecca nor William had any intention whatsoever to challenge any appraisal. Despite knowing that Mr. Plaintiffs' Attorney was actively misrepresenting their goals, Rebecca and William had no means to correct the fallacy.

No Discussion about Payment of Property Taxes

During this hearing, Rebecca asked about property taxes, and specifically how the property taxes would be paid. Rebecca and William had suggested months earlier to Mr. Plaintiffs' Attorney that each of the plaintiffs mail their respective payments to Mr. Plaintiffs' Attorney, and the two defendants would do the same. To bring the taxes current, Mr. Plaintiffs' Attorney could forward the five payments to the tax assessor. But Mr. Plaintiffs' Attorney had ignored their suggestion.

Although Rebecca asked the question, there was no discussion about the payment of taxes during the hearing.

Defendants' Perspective to Date

The Honorable Mr. Impartial had explained during an earlier hearing that property taxes would be paid from the sale of the property.

So, the fact that there was no discussion about property taxes during this hearing implied that the result of the case would be the sale of the property to a third party. While this did not come as a surprise to Rebecca or William, they were still being led to believe that negotiation was possible. Mr. Plaintiffs' Attorney continued to state that he felt that a settlement was near, but he also consistently refused a discussion with the defendants.

The numerous contradictions in Mr. Plaintiffs' Attorney's approach confused the defendants. They still believed that the appraisers were going to meet and awaited that meeting to take place.

From May 2013 through September 2013, Rebecca sent email after email to Mr. Plaintiffs' Attorney asking that he respond to their questions. Rebecca and William continued to ask him questions about multiple topics and copied the court each time.

Among the questions that Rebecca and William asked were: Will the plaintiffs pay each of their shares of the property taxes and when will they pay? Had the third appraisal been completed? If, so when will the three appraisers (Ms. Low Appraiser, Ms. High Appraiser, and Mr. Third Appraiser) meet? What is the agenda for the appraisers' meeting? When will the three appraisers discuss their findings with Rebecca and William? What is the plaintiffs' alleged buyer's offer? When will the plaintiffs send documentation of the plaintiffs' buyer's offer to Rebecca and William? When can Rebecca and William expect to receive any documentation for review?

Rebecca and William also continued to ask questions such as: What is the court process for the partition? Do the plaintiffs want to sell the property by listing the property or by an auction? If the property is listed, will the price be adjusted at intervals if no buyer comes forward? What is the plaintiffs' plan to maintain the property? Will the plaintiffs agree to at least maintain the lawn? And finally, Rebecca and William asked what creative options do each of the plaintiffs have that they might share with the defendants?

As had been the case throughout the lawsuit, Mr. Plaintiffs' Attorney did not respond in any form to Rebecca's questions.

The progress of the lawsuit seemed to have stalled. The path that the lawsuit took was still outside of the control of both Rebecca and William. Neither knew what actions they could take to move the process forward. Since the plaintiffs had not stated their specific expectations, the defendants believed that the case could continue indefinitely. They still hoped that the plaintiffs would back down and drop the lawsuit. But the longer the case dragged on, the more doubtful were the defendants. Rebecca and William could only guess as to what would happen next.

While Rebecca and William waited for a new hearing to be scheduled, Rebecca emailed Ms. High Appraiser to learn her perspective about how Mr. Plaintiffs' Attorney had obtained the appraisal that Rebecca and William had hired her to complete. Since Ms. High Appraiser worked for a realtor and Rebecca had hired her to complete the appraisal, Rebecca expected that Ms. High Appraiser would have immediately contacted her about Mr. Plaintiffs'

Attorney's communication with her as a professional courtesy. But Ms. High Appraiser hadn't contacted Rebecca.

After a couple of weeks, Rebecca received an email from Ms. High Appraiser. Ms. High Appraiser explained that Mr. Plaintiffs' Attorney had contacted her and asked her to give him the results of the appraisal. At first, Ms. High Appraiser explained, she refused to give him the results. According to Ms. High Appraiser, Mr. Plaintiffs' Attorney then threatened to subpoena her to a court hundreds of miles from the city where the property is located if she did not tell him the results of her appraisal. So, rather than being forced to travel to the distant location in response to Mr. Plaintiffs' Attorney's threatened subpoena, Ms. High Appraiser instead gave him the results. Ms. High Appraiser didn't elaborate on her reasons for keeping the matter to herself.

While Ms. High Appraiser's explanation provided answers to minor questions, Rebecca still wondered why Mr. Plaintiffs' Attorney had gone to such extreme measures rather than simply communicating with the defendants.

Why hadn't Mr. Plaintiffs' attorney simply asked Rebecca for the information? What had been his purpose in contacting Ms. High Appraiser? Why would he have subpoenaed her to appear at a location hundreds of miles from the court where the case is being heard? An entirely different judge would have presided in a different jurisdiction. Is that legal?

Fourth Reason the Case Took Years to Complete

The fourth reason that the lawsuit took over two years to complete was Mr. Plaintiffs' Attorney's refusal to respond to Rebecca's and William's questions. Rebecca and William waited months for answers to the most basic questions. In some cases, they were never given answers. Although Rebecca and William had no control over the legal process, as equal property owners, they had a right to know information that pertained to the sale of the property.

Rebecca contacted the court to complain that the process had stalled and that it appeared that Mr. Plaintiffs' Attorney was avoiding settlement. She copied Mr. Plaintiffs' Attorney on her letter.

A few weeks later, Rebecca and William each received a notice that a new hearing had been scheduled for October 31, 2013, Halloween.

Chapter X – Trial Brief

Ten days before the scheduled October 31, 2013, hearing that was titled a trial, Rebecca submitted to the court and Mr. Plaintiffs' Attorney the Defendants' Trial Brief.

The Definition of a Trial Brief

The definition of a *trial brief* (Trial brief, 2015) is: "A document prepared for and used by an attorney at trial which contains, among other things, issues to be tried, synopsis of evidence and witnesses to be presented, and case and statutory authority for the position of counsel at trial."

The Definition of American Rule

According to Investopedia, the definition of *American rule* is: "A rule in law and economics that says attorney fees should be paid by each party involved in litigation - even the party that wins the case" (American Rule, 2015).

Another source defines American rule as: "A legal rule controlling assessment of attorney's fees arising out of litigation. The American rule provides that each party is responsible for paying its own attorney's fees unless specific authority granted by statute or contract allows the assessment of those fees against the other party (American rule (attorney's fees), 2015).

Defendants' Trial Brief

Rebecca's and William's Defendants' Trial Brief was direct, powerful and most of all, based on factual events. Within the document, Rebecca reiterated the numerous points that she and William had expressed throughout the course of the lawsuit. The defendants had made repeated attempts to communicate with both Mr. Plaintiffs' Attorney and the plaintiffs in multiple ways, the defendants had offered to purchase the property and to negotiate a settlement, and the defendants had also agreed to a sale based on the Competitive Market Analysis. Rebecca added that this is a no-fault case. Regarding payment of attorney fees, she referenced the American Rule.

She also stated that the plaintiffs had refused a discussion of non-legal options toward settlement.

In an expression of her opinion, Rebecca voiced that the plaintiffs had filed the lawsuit with the purpose of harming the defendants by attempting to force them to pay the plaintiffs' presumably enormous attorney fees. Rebecca reasoned that hiring attorneys would not have been needed had a non-legal agreement been discussed and finalized. In her Answer, Rebecca had requested that the plaintiffs drop their lawsuit.

Plaintiffs' Attorney's Trial Brief

Mr. Plaintiffs' Attorney included in his trial brief numerous statements that apparently were meant to mislead the judge. He stated his perspective that the defendants were unwilling to compensate the plaintiffs, and "the siblings' relationship has deteriorated to the point where they barely speak to each other, and in fact, there is real animosity amongst them."

Mr. Plaintiffs' Attorney grossly exaggerated the condition of the buildings with statements such as "a decaying cottage" and "the cottage and garage are in dire need of renovation just to make it usable." He stated that the property should be sold at auction.

Next, Mr. Plaintiffs' Attorney suggested in the trial brief that, "Defendants were not satisfied with Ms. High

Appraiser's appraiser so they then hired Ms. Low Appraiser with the hopes that the second appraisal would be more to their liking."

He finished his argument with the statement, "No formal offers have been made because of the prospective purchaser's knowledge that the defendants do not wish to sell at this time."

Defendants' Issues with Plaintiffs' Attorney's Trial Brief

In Rebecca's opinion, the grave problem with Mr. Plaintiffs' Attorney's trial brief was the numerous false statements. Rebecca reminded herself that Mr. Plaintiffs' Attorney's approach was adversarial. She found his statements to be unbelievable and intentionally misleading.

Mr. Plaintiffs' Attorney's statement that "there is animosity amongst them" implied two-way animosity. It didn't specify that any animosity demonstrated was only on the parts of the three plaintiffs, and not on the parts of either Rebecca or William. Rebecca and William remain perplexed as to their sisters' reasons for their extreme hostility and their refusal to communicate with them.

Further, Mr. Plaintiffs' Attorney didn't mention that Rebecca had initiated the mediation. Nor had he described Rebecca's and William's numerous attempts to communicate with their sisters prior to and after their sisters' filing of the lawsuit.

Rebecca recalled that Mr. Plaintiffs' Attorney had negatively described the property buildings as rustic in January 2013 to Rebecca and William following the pre-trial hearing. While in need of roof repair and general maintenance, not a renovation, both structures were and remain both usable. It seemed odd to Rebecca that Mr. Plaintiffs' Attorney would intentionally mischaracterize the condition of the buildings since he wanted the appraisals to be high.

Mr. Plaintiffs' Attorney's argument to sell the property at an auction is the second most extreme option possible next to allowing foreclosure. It does not take an expert to know that the sale price for such an action could be extremely low allowing the winner of the auction to get a bargain, but at a substantial loss to the sellers. It seemed that his was an all-or-nothing approach, that he expected the defendants to buy-out the plaintiffs at $250,000, or he desired the property to be sold at auction.

Ms. Low Appraiser and Ms. High Appraiser completed their respective appraisals within the same 24-hour period, also a fact of which Mr. Plaintiffs' Attorney was well aware. Rebecca and William did not receive the results of Ms. Low Appraiser's appraisal for at least a week and longer for the second appraisal.

Mr. Plaintiffs' Attorney was further well aware that both Rebecca and William had agreed to sell in their Answers and before The Honorable Mr. Impartial in January 2013. Therefore Mr. Plaintiffs' Attorney's statement, "no formal offers have been made because of the prospective purchaser's knowledge that the defendants do not wish to sell at this time" appeared to be nothing short of a manipulation of statements, deliberately misleading and taking facts out of context.

Since Mr. Plaintiffs' Attorney had not come forth with information about the plaintiffs' alleged buyer, the defendants still didn't know if a buyer existed. Rebecca and William also pondered how a prospective buyer could believe that the "defendants do not wish to sell at this time" unless Mr. Plaintiffs' Attorney had communicated the erroneous statement to them or the plaintiffs themselves were the plaintiffs' alleged buyers.

Finally, Rebecca and William were very willing to compensate their sisters. They based their proposed starting price on a valid appraisal. Both believed the price was reasonable. The property was in need of repairs.

Also, Rebecca took into consideration the significant amount of money that their sisters had spent from their parent's estate during their forced probate case against their parent over a decade earlier. Marta and Barbara are the primaries responsible for instigating that action which paid their lawyers and others hundreds of thousands of dollars. Initiated without their parent's, Rebecca's or William's knowledge, and without caring if Rebecca and William agreed, Marta's and Barbara's probate legal action cost their parent approximately $500,000. The subsequent loss to Rebecca's and William's inheritance was each approximately $100,000 minus their parent's care. During the last ten years of Rebecca's and William's parent's life, expenses paid for their parent's care were minimal compared to payments made to attorneys, guardians, the Conservator, and others.

Although this court would not have taken the lost inheritance into consideration, Rebecca idealistically felt that her sisters might feel conscience-driven to compensate them. That would have been a topic of conversation had Rebecca been able to speak directly with each of the plaintiffs.

Rebecca and William had made a formal offer and still expected that the appraisers would meet so that a mutually agreed price could be determined through amicable, informal discussion.

It seemed that Mr. Plaintiffs' Attorney's attempts to twist the truth of Rebecca's and William's efforts to negotiate, and his apparent constantly shifting objectives simply added to the confusion.

Plaintiff's Second Scheduling Conflict

Prior to the October 31st hearing, Mr. Plaintiffs' Attorney stated in an email that Marta had a new scheduling conflict and to accommodate her schedule as a professional courtesy, he would ask for an adjournment of the trial. The Plaintiffs' Attorney explained that Marta "cannot be present due to some academic obligations." Mr. Plaintiffs' Attorney had stated prior to the mediation that his client would appear if there was a trial.

Would the court accept the motion to accommodate the plaintiff, the primary initiator of the lawsuit?

Plaintiffs' Attorney Files Plaintiffs' Ex-Parte Motion for Adjournment of Trial

Although Marta had filed the lawsuit, it seemed again that it was not a priority to her to attend hearings and especially a trial. On October 29, 2013, The Plaintiffs' Attorney filed a *Plaintiffs' Ex-Parte Motion for Adjournment of Trial*.

Plaintiffs' Attorney Suggests Off-Location Meeting

In a flurry of emails that preceded the hearing, Mr. Plaintiffs' Attorney suggested that "we at least make an attempt at settlement." Rebecca and William still had not received responses from Mr. Plaintiffs' Attorney to their numerous questions. The case was now over one-and-one-half years old.

Mr. Plaintiffs' Attorney suggested that Rebecca and William meet with him at a location hundreds of miles from the location of the property. This was an unusual request since Rebecca and William could have both connected by teleconference call as an alternative to meeting at the courthouse near the property. And if Mr. Plaintiffs' Attorney had documentation for Rebecca's and William's review, he could have emailed that to both defendants.

Defendants' Perspective of Meeting at Off-Location

Pros

Rebecca and William considered that they might be able to obtain some answers to the many questions that they had regularly asked Mr. Plaintiffs' Attorney. They still expected that the appraisers would meet.

Cons

Mr. Plaintiffs' Attorney's recurring statement that "we should at least attempt settlement" appeared to be another deliberate attempt to mislead the court. Since he had not responded to the defendants' questions, Rebecca and William were perplexed as to Mr. Plaintiffs' Attorney's intent as it was their opinion that Mr. Plaintiffs' Attorney still hadn't seriously attempted to settle at all.

Mr. Plaintiffs' Attorney had not offered any specific details about his agenda that were significantly different than those previously discussed months earlier at the second hearing. It appeared that his clients still demanded the high appraisal amount. The promise of compromise seemed to be only a bluff.

Although the plaintiffs had agreed to pay each of their three shares of the property taxes, they still had not made any attempt to do so to date. Also, there had been no further discussion about payment of attorney fees.

Rebecca asked again that Mr. Plaintiffs' Attorney respond to her questions. What terms would be different than those that Mr. Plaintiffs' Attorney discussed at the mediation? Did Mr. Plaintiffs' Attorney still expect that Rebecca and William each agree to pay one fifth of his attorney fees? How would the property be maintained if the defendants didn't buy it?

Did Mr. Plaintiffs' Attorney intend to attempt to force the defendants to unconditionally agree to his terms or to otherwise coerce them in some way? And if the defendants did not agree, was Mr. Plaintiffs' Attorney's intention to declare to the court that the defendants had refused settlement?

Both defendants were perplexed as to the reason Mr. Plaintiffs' Attorney suggested meeting at an alternative location. They speculated if there was an unspoken reason that Mr. Plaintiffs' Attorney proposed meeting at the distant location rather than simply having a teleconference call with the two defendants or through email communication. Had the buildings been demolished without their knowledge? Nothing seemed too far-fetched at this point. Rebecca wanted to check on the property.

Defendants' Perspective to Date:

Rebecca preferred that any meeting take place at the courthouse where the property is located. Mr. Plaintiffs' Attorney's suggestion to meet at the off-location made no sense to her. She had previously requested that all communications be in written form so that William and she could together review information before responding. But Mr. Plaintiffs' Attorney seemed reluctant to state much in writing.

Was Mr. Plaintiffs' Attorney suddenly attempting to avoid a trial? By filing the lawsuit, isn't a trial what the plaintiffs wanted all along? It appeared that Mr. Plaintiffs' Attorney planned to present an ultimatum. Rebecca doubted that Mr. Plaintiffs' Attorney intended any reciprocal discussion.

With the question of payment of attorney fees still undecided, Rebecca thought that the American Rule would apply. She was adamantly against agreeing to pay part of Mr. Plaintiffs' Attorney's legal fees, especially since she still had no idea of his charges to date. But that the defendants pay his fees seemed to be a matter of great importance to Mr. Plaintiffs' Attorney.

Not being a lawyer, Rebecca was not aware of the applicability or significance of a statute. She knew that neither William nor she had done anything wrong. But Rebecca felt a gnawing ache, the impact of not knowing what the future holds. Would William and she be forced to pay their sisters' attorney fees simply because Marta had filed the lawsuit? Didn't there need to be a reason to award attorney fees?

Rebecca and William awaited the appraiser meeting. They had no reason to believe that the appraiser meeting would not take place. They had not been told of any new developments despite their numerous attempts to obtain answers. They still believed that the appraisers who would be meeting would be Ms. Low Appraiser, Ms. High Appraiser, and Mr. Third Appraiser. Rebecca and William had received the information that Mr. Third Appraiser's appraisal results were also $250,000, the same as Ms. High Appraiser's results.

By this time, Mr. Plaintiffs' Attorney had vaguely responded that his answers depended on whether or not the defendants purchased the property. Rebecca realized that Mr. Plaintiffs' Attorney wasn't considering settlement topics concurrently. Instead, it appeared now that he was attempting to force the defendants to buy-out the plaintiffs. It further looked as if Mr. Plaintiffs' Attorney was deliberately avoiding negotiation.

Rebecca and William had already declined to accept the plaintiffs' counter-offer of $235, 000. Did the plaintiffs now expect the defendants to buy them out at $250,000 with no other plan in mind but foreclosure or sale by an auction? The plaintiffs had not counter-offered that the defendants purchase the property at the higher amount of $250,000. So, the defendants weren't given the opportunity to decline the offer so that negotiation could proceed. The case had become a tangled web.

Rebecca and William decided to attend the hearing as scheduled rather than meet with Mr. Plaintiffs' Attorney at a distant location. They didn't know if the court had accepted Mr. Plaintiffs' Attorney's Motion for Adjournment or not.

They expected a similar meeting to those that had already taken place with, as usual, The Honorable Mr. Impartial presiding. Rebecca and William were in for several surprises.

Chapter XI – Trial or Settlement Conference?

New Participant

The Honorable Mr. Reasonable

New Judge

Rebecca and William recognized upon entering a new courtroom that The Honorable Mr. Impartial was not present and a different judge, The Honorable Mr. Reasonable would hear this meeting.

Neither Rebecca nor William knew whether the meeting was to be considered a trial or a settlement conference.

Plaintiffs' Attorney's Whispered Statement

Prior to the start of the October 31, 2013 hearing, Mr. Plaintiffs' Attorney whispered to Rebecca that the three appraisers would testify. She interpreted the statement as threatening due to the menacing manner in which Mr. Plaintiffs' Attorney addressed her. Once again, Rebecca had not challenged any appraisal. It seemed odd that Mr. Plaintiffs' Attorney had singled her out rather than addressing both William and her.

Ms. Low Appraiser Not Present

Rebecca immediately observed that Ms. Low Appraiser was not present. Mr. Third Appraiser introduced himself to Rebecca and William. A fourth appraiser, Mr. Plaintiffs' Attorney's Appraiser whom Rebecca and William had not met stood off to the side. Ms. High Appraiser stood next to Mr. Plaintiffs' Attorney's Appraiser. Rebecca had expected a hearing, not a trial, so she had not subpoenaed or asked Ms. Low Appraiser to attend. It was clear that Mr. Plaintiffs' Attorney had been instrumental in securing the attendance of the other appraisers. Apparently, Mr. Plaintiffs' Attorney expected and prepared for a trial.

Defendants' Perspective

As Rebecca and William entered the courtroom, they began to realize that they had been unashamedly deceived. If an appraiser meeting had taken place, it clearly hadn't included Ms. Low Appraiser. It was also obvious that Mr. Plaintiffs' Attorney had never intended that Ms. Low Appraiser would be included. To Rebecca and William, it appeared too late that Ms. Low Appraiser meet with the other appraisers.

Enormously disappointed at what Rebecca and William recognized as an act of direct and deliberate deception, Rebecca and William felt the profound emotional impact that they were about to lose their beloved property forever. There would be no negotiation toward a middle ground. There was no hope for compromise. Mr. Plaintiffs' Attorney had escalated the contest to the next level.

Settlement Discussion with Judge

Rebecca, William, and Mr. Plaintiffs' Attorney met briefly and informally with The Honorable Mr. Reasonable. The judge was dressed in street clothes. The judge directed his initial comments to Rebecca stating, "I read your trial brief."

Rebecca felt uncomfortable, somewhat under scrutiny and singled out. She wondered if the judge had read any of the multiple other documents that William and she had sent to the court, their respective Answers, their multiple letters to Mr. Plaintiffs' Attorney and the court, and the fact that she had initiated mediation. There was a reason the judge was addressing Rebecca so abruptly. She had no idea of the reason though and was hesitant to speculate or make assumptions.

Since Rebecca had re-read Mr. Plaintiffs' Attorney's trial brief again the night before, she mentally recalled points that he made. Rebecca was still shocked by Mr. Plaintiffs' Attorney's numerous inaccurate statements. It appeared that the plaintiffs' attorney had placed Rebecca as his primary target. Mr. Plaintiffs' Attorney had stated in his trial brief that the defendants are unwilling to sell. Was the judge basing his perspective on that statement and the other comments that Mr. Plaintiffs' Attorney had made?

The Honorable Mr. Reasonable then stated to both Rebecca and William, "I'll give the defendants some time to discuss what they want to do. Make a final decision."

Final Discussion Between Defendants

The judge and Mr. Plaintiffs' Attorney both left the room leaving Rebecca and William to ponder their last chance to save their beloved property. They now had two choices, either to sell or to buy at the high appraisal price of $250,000, really the only option that they had all along while they were led to believe that negotiation could occur.

Rebecca and William still did not know the outcome of who would pay attorney fees. Nor did they know if the plaintiffs would pay each of their shares of the property taxes. So, the price that they would be considering could easily have approached $275,000 or higher.

The decision about the property was an all-or-nothing choice. There would be no compromise or further discussion. That was painfully obvious.

They also knew that their sisters demanded payment in cash since Mr. Plaintiffs' Attorney had requested in mediation that the defendants supply him with each of their financial records. Payment in cash is an action to which very few buyers except the financially wealthiest would agree. That topic also had not been discussed.

With the cards stacked against them, the two defendants agreed once more that they had no other choice at this time than to give up their beloved lakefront property.

It was possible but improbable that the defendants still could have owned the property. That outcome was dependent upon the future progress of the case. If a buyer didn't materialize, would the plaintiffs have chosen foreclosure leading possibly to the complete loss of the property? Foreclosure for failure to pay property taxes would have become an issue before an auction could have been scheduled. Could the attorney have requested that the state delay foreclosure? Would the judge accept the offer that the defendants had proposed instead of ordering a sale by an auction? Or did the legal procedure rules require the judge to automatically order an auction?

The majority of the questions were up to the judge to decide if the matter came to that.

Settlement Hearing

The judge, still wearing street clothes and Mr. Plaintiffs' Attorney re-entered the room. The Honorable Mr. Reasonable asked for Rebecca's and William's decision. Yet one more time, Rebecca and William each stated, "I agree to sell." The Honorable Mr. Reasonable stated, "That's what I would have decided."

The Honorable Mr. Reasonable's Statements

The Honorable Mr. Reasonable excused himself and returned a few minutes later wearing his robe. He had requested that the clerk take the minutes. At each of the other hearings, no minutes were taken.

The formal hearing began as the judge again covered the details of the case. The property would be listed by a realtor at the appraisal price of $250,000. There was additional discussion about filing motions for attorney fees at a later date. Mr. Plaintiffs' Attorney stated, "In the event that it does go to a sale, we would be willing to bring our motion for attorney fees and costs." Rebecca noted the attorney's curious use of the phrase "would be willing."

The judge stated, "If I were to settle this case today, myself, you know, I would find both parties equally at fault and probably not award attorney fees and costs . . . I'm not going to make that decision. I'm going to let The Honorable Mr. Impartial make that decision." He also warned the defendants that regarding the statute in the American Rule, "The Honorable Mr. Impartial might rule that 'the statute allows for the party bringing the action for sale and partition' . . . You are aware that the court might rule against you."

The Honorable Mr. Impartial didn't explain the reasons or how the defendants might lose such a ruling against them. Nor did he explain how he believed both parties to be equally at fault or why he wasn't going to award attorney fees and costs on that day.

The defendants had agreed to sell and had not contested anything. Rebecca and William didn't understand how either of them could be perceived as being at fault. Except that Mr. Plaintiffs' Attorney had made false and misleading statements.

Defendants' Perspective to Date

Rebecca and William left the meeting feeling a range of emotions. They had been deceived by Mr. Plaintiffs' Attorney about issues that could have been resolved months earlier. Had Mr. Plaintiffs' Attorney stated at the pre-trial hearing that the plaintiffs would only accept the highest appraisal obtained and were not willing to negotiate, one-and-one-half years of legal action could have been avoided.

Rather than having the appraisers meet toward negotiation, Mr. Plaintiffs' Attorney's suspected purpose was confirmed to instead create the impression of majority rule among the appraisers to the judge. And he intended that the appraisers testify at trial in an adversarial manner although the defendants had never challenged any appraisal.

Mr. Plaintiffs' Attorney's twisting of truths and miss-statements seemed to be a tactic for some purpose. Rebecca and William could not figure who it would serve. In any event, Mr. Plaintiffs' Attorney, Rebecca, and William weren't on the same page as far as an interpretation of events went. Rebecca believed that Mr. Plaintiffs' Attorney was well aware and encouraged miscommunication.

Rebecca and William didn't learn why The Honorable Mr. Reasonable had substituted for The Honorable Mr. Impartial, yet knew that The Honorable Mr. Impartial's absence was beyond their control. Either judge could have scheduled the hearing. And perhaps, the hearing could have been rescheduled at a time to coincide with The Honorable Mr. Impartial's schedule though that did not occur.

Could an attorney have requested that the hearing be rescheduled? Yes, probably, since Mr. Plaintiffs' Attorney had successfully requested and been granted an adjournment. But Rebecca and William still did not have legal representation.

Chapter XII – Ordering a Transcript

The Definition of a Transcript

The definition of a *transcript* (Transcript, 2015) is: "the written record of all proceedings, including testimony, in a trial, hearing or deposition."

How to Order a Transcript

Rebecca telephoned the court and asked the process to obtain a copy of the court transcript. The receptionist transferred her to the clerk who told her to telephone the Court Transcriptionist, a Certified Electronic Recorder so that her request could be added to her schedule. That person advised Rebecca to send a check for the transcript, and when it was completed, she would mail a copy of the transcript to Rebecca.

Chapter XIII – Defendant Hires an Attorney

New Participant:

Mr. Defendant's Attorney

Example of Right of First Refusal

Collett (March, 2011), offered this example of *Right of First Refusal*: "Owner A owns a parcel of real estate that she wants to sell to Purchaser B for $1,000,000 under certain terms and conditions. However, Holder C has a right of first refusal to purchase the real estate. Before Owner A can sell the real estate to Purchaser B, she must first offer it to Holder C under the same terms and conditions as those offered by Purchaser B. If Holder C exercises the right of first refusal and follows through with the purchase, Purchaser B will have no right to acquire the real estate."

Defendants' Perspective to Date

Rebecca remembered the key points of the hearing such as Right of First Refusal and that a statute might apply to the American Rule. Although she understood that it was imperative that an attorney explain to her how a statute was relevant to the rule, she still had been advised by other attorneys in a general sense that each party usually pays their fees. Generally speaking, despite the fact that she felt dissected under The Honorable Mr. Reasonable's initial suspicious glare, she felt relatively comfortable with the outcome of this meeting. It had been a settlement hearing and had not turned into a trial. But at the time, she wasn't sure.

Rebecca and William remained firm in their perspective that they wanted a non-adversarial solution. However, they had felt that they were expected to give up each of their shares and to accept Mr. Plaintiffs' Attorney's services as their own as a condition of settlement. They did not understand the apparent expectation that they must accept Mr. Plaintiffs' Attorney as their attorney. They also knew that they each had rights as co-owners of the property.

Rebecca determined that much of the seeming complexity of the situation was due to not having an attorney. She was not well-informed about legal terms, and she didn't know how to respond to statements made by the judge. Nor did she know what motions to file. Mainly she wondered how she could correct many false statements that she believed others had made, and finally expose the truth. Rebecca felt that she was at a definite disadvantage. She knew that it was imperative that she obtain legal counsel.

Rebecca weighed her understanding of what had taken place during the hearing. William and she needed assistance in several areas. There were the primary questions of payment of attorney fees and payment of property taxes. Although the plaintiffs seemed remarkably unconcerned, Rebecca had begun to receive delinquent payment notices for the taxes. There remained the risk of foreclosure even though the case was in the court system. And even if the property was listed, there was no guarantee that a buyer would come forward. Then the matter would still be decided by the court, and probably sell at auction. Rebecca wasn't clear as to the benefit of Right of First Refusal. Would that help or hurt William and her? She wasn't sure.

Rebecca decided that it was time to hire an attorney.

How to Choose an Attorney

Over a year earlier, Rebecca had researched a dozen attorneys. Now, she wondered who she could find that would take a case that had been in progress for over one-and-one-half years. She eliminated from her list attorneys who charge by the hour. Additionally, Rebecca focused on attorneys whose offices are located within a twenty-five-mile radius of the location of the property. She also wanted to hire an attorney having special expertise and experience with partition lawsuits who could guide her through the process.

As Rebecca conversed with each lawyer, many advised her to find an attorney within the town where the property is located. She hadn't considered travel costs to and from hearings.

Attorney Fees

Rebecca learned that attorneys charge in different ways. The four different ways that fees are typically charged are hourly rates, flat fees, retainers and contingent fees (How, and How Much, Do Lawyers Charge, 2015) .

While an hourly rate initially might seem affordable, attorneys can charge anywhere from $200 to $500 per hour depending upon their level of experience and where they work. Charges can include everything from attendance at hearings to travel expenses to telephone calls to reading emails. Costs are usually billed at additional rates. In general, one can estimate what a final charge might be within a wide range. Once all of the billing is calculated based on an hourly rate, the final charge could be $10,000 to $20,000 for a non-contested lawsuit, more or less. "An experienced lawyer will be able to better estimate how many lawyer hours a particular matter will take to resolve" (How, and How Much, Do Lawyers Charge, 2015).

The second fee arrangement is that an attorney might charge a flat fee or a one-time charge. If the lawyer agrees to charge a flat fee, it is wise to ask the attorney to specify precisely what services the fee will cover. The attorney may add a clause to the contract that additional fees might be warranted, however with a discussion with the client. Be sure to read any contract before signing it. Attorneys charge flat fees for cases that are usually easily resolved such as "wills, uncontested divorces and simple bankruptcy filings" (How, and How Much, Do Lawyers Charge, 2015).

Some lawyers charge a retainer fee. The amount of a retainer fee can be anywhere from $1000 on up, but many fall within the range of $2500 - $3500. The client agrees to pay the attorney the retainer fee to begin to work on the case. As the case progresses, the attorney deducts the costs of services from the retainer fee. Once the retainer fee is exhausted, the attorney will ask for a new retainer fee or may bill by another form of payment depending on the terms of the contract or the attorney's preference. So, the rate per hour might end up at a cost that is significantly more than an hourly fee. As with paying an hourly rate, the final fees might fall within the range of $10,000 to $20,000, more or less.

The last type of fee arrangement is on a contingent basis. That means that the attorney will take "a percentage, typically one-third (1/3) of the settlement or money upon a judgment . . . Used typically for medical malpractice, personal injury cases or debt collection cases" (How, and How Much, Do Lawyers Charge, 2015). If an attorney suggests this arrangement for a partition lawsuit, it would be wise to check with other attorneys to see if this form of payment is allowed by law with family cases.

For any and all billing, be sure to "ask your attorney to include in the fee agreement a provision for periodic, itemized billing" (How, and How Much, Do Lawyers

Charge, 2015). If you ask for itemized billing, you'll receive a long list of the actual items billed and the charge for each. Why is this important?

Attorneys might unintentionally double-bill or might bill for services that didn't occur. For example, if an attorney's bill lists charges for telephone calls when you've never had a telephone conversation with the attorney, one can dispute that part of the bill. Also, if the attorney works for a law firm, a junior attorney might perform some tasks. Be sure that you know which attorney is performing which tasks to be sure that you are not overcharged. Asking for an itemized billing allows the client to check that what is billed is in order.

At the time that Rebecca was researching attorneys, she knew only about hourly rates, flat rates, and retainer fees. It's important to understand the ramifications of agreeing to a form of payment. Based on Rebecca's and William's experience with the Involuntary Guardianship that their sisters had filed against their parent over a decade earlier, and the attorney fees charged to their parent's estate, they were well aware that attorney costs could escalate out of control in this case. They both felt that they had kept their costs down up to this point. At the same time, they could only estimate a final bill without having knowledge of the variables related to Mr. Plaintiffs' Attorney's fees and costs so far. His fees could have been anywhere from $10,000 to as high as $50,000. But those were kept secret from them.

After Rebecca requested recommendations, several attorneys suggested one lawyer whose office is within a mile of the courthouse. Rebecca had communicated with him earlier in the case. When she contacted him, she was relieved to hear that he remembered her inquiry and would take the case. The attorney, Mr. Defendant's Attorney, charged a flat rate that was reasonable to Rebecca.

Rebecca's decision to hire Mr. Defendant's Attorney in November 2013 was based on two factors. First that he charged a flat fee allowed her to keep her legal costs down. Second, the attorney's law office is located within walking distance of the courthouse. In small towns, professionals know each other well. If nothing else, the professionals in the town where the property is located are acquaintances and had known each other for years.

Rebecca had interviewed two other attorneys with offices in the same town. The first asked an expensive amount for a retainer fee. The second appeared to distrust her as a potential client because she lived out of state, and also required payment of a steep retainer fee.

She chose the attorney who she believed would work toward her advantage. This was an unnecessarily complicated case. Other attorneys had refused to accept the case. They stated that they worked too far from the location of the property and their attendance at multiple hearings would be required. But, it was clear that Mr. Defendant's Attorney contemplated that the case could be easily and swiftly resolved. Rebecca felt that she made a good choice in selecting an attorney.

Communications with Defendants' Attorney

After Rebecca hired Mr. Defendant's Attorney, she brought him up to speed on the hearings and events that had taken place to date. Most importantly, as soon as Rebecca received the transcript of the October 31, 2013 hearing, she immediately sent it to him for review.

Mr. Defendant's Attorney had asked Rebecca several times if the hearing had been a settlement or a trial. With the transcript in hand, he developed a plan to proceed.

Although Rebecca frequently asked Mr. Defendant's Attorney questions, she kept her general discussions with him short. The majority of her communications with her attorney were in email form.

Tax Notices

In addition to asking questions, Rebecca regularly sent Mr. Defendant's Attorney copies of the delinquent tax notices that she received in the mail.

Rebecca stopped emailing Mr. Plaintiffs' Attorney and instead relied on Mr. Defendant's Attorney to converse with the plaintiffs' attorney.

Property Not Listed

Besides the ongoing issue with non-payment of the taxes, Rebecca also observed that the property had not been listed even though Mr. Plaintiffs' Attorney had requested that action during the formal October 31, 2013 hearing.

Ms. Realtor One was the realtor that Mr. Plaintiffs' Attorney, Rebecca, and William, and the court had mutually agreed to be used. Rebecca regularly accessed Ms. Realtor One's realtor's website and independent realtor websites in case the listing appeared. She saw no sign of a listing. Why hadn't the property been listed yet?

Communications with Plaintiffs

Since Rebecca was receiving the delinquent tax notices on an almost monthly basis, she decided to attempt again to contact each of her sisters directly to warn them of the seriousness of not paying the property taxes with the threat of foreclosure looming.

Chapter XIV – The Judge's Ruling

On March 6, 2014, The Honorable Mr. Impartial ruled on the case regarding attorney fees. The judge ruled that the plaintiffs and defendants would each pay their attorney fees.

After years of apprehension about payment of attorney fees, Rebecca and William were thankful and relieved that The Honorable Mr. Impartial made the decision that he did.

Yes, Rebecca and William took a risk when neither hired an attorney earlier, but better late than never. Rebecca was confident that Mr. Defendant's Attorney successfully argued in their favor and was instrumental in achieving their goal that the plaintiffs pay their attorney fees.

One would think that the case was probably over at this point. Well, no. There were still more surprises to come.

Chapter XV – The Selection of a New Realtor

Two months later, on May 7, 2014, Mr. Defendant's Attorney emailed Rebecca that Mr. Plaintiffs' Attorney was going to allow Mr. Defendant's Attorney and her to select a new realtor. Ms. Realtor One still had not listed the property.

Rebecca did not know why Ms. Realtor One had not listed the property and did not ask the reason. That the case seemed to be again moving forward was a relief to her.

For Rebecca's selection, she immediately chose Mr. Realtor Two, the employer of Ms. High Appraiser, the appraiser that Rebecca and William had hired to complete one of their two appraisals. Although Rebecca was still curious as to why Ms. High Appraiser had not contacted her when Mr. Plaintiff's Attorney demanded that she provide him the results of her appraisal, Rebecca nevertheless decided that it was a good choice. Mr. Plaintiffs' Attorney had either requested or subpoenaed Ms. High Appraiser to testify at the October 31, 2013 hearing. Rebecca believed that he and the three plaintiffs would be in agreement with her selection.

Rebecca and William never learned why Ms. Realtor One had not listed the property. Over six months passed from the time that the court approved that Ms. Realtor One list the property to the time that a new realtor was selected. A sale had not progressed as a result. The realtor had not conversed with either Rebecca or William.

On June 12, 2014, Mr. Defendant's Attorney emailed Rebecca that he had sent a listing agreement to Mr. Plaintiffs' Attorney for the plaintiffs' signatures.

New Participant

Mr. Realtor Two

Chapter XVI – Plaintiffs No Longer Represented by Attorney

Later that month in June of 2014, Mr. Defendant's Attorney emailed Rebecca that Mr. Plaintiffs' Attorney no longer represented the three plaintiffs.

As with other developments, Rebecca and William did not learn the reason for Mr. Plaintiffs' Attorney's departure. The plaintiffs either released him or he quit the case.

They could only guess as to the reasons for the action.

In any event, the three plaintiffs no longer had legal counsel. As far as Rebecca knew, the plaintiffs had not hired a new attorney.

And if the plaintiffs had hired a new attorney, they had not informed Mr. Defendant's Attorney.

Chapter XVII – Plaintiffs Refuse to List Property

Mr. Defendant's Attorney emailed Rebecca that the three plaintiffs had refused to sign the listing agreement with Mr. Realtor Two.

Once again, Rebecca and William didn't know the reasons for their sisters' refusal. They only knew that their three sisters had not signed the listing agreement.

On July 2, 2014, Mr. Defendant's Attorney sent the listing agreement to Rebecca. Rebecca signed the agreement to finally get the property listed. At this time, Rebecca accepted sole responsibility for the listing. She reasoned that if the property didn't get listed, they would miss the opportunity of informing potential buyers of its availability during the important warm summer months.

The next day, Mr. Defendant's Attorney forwarded Rebecca's signed listing agreement to Mr. Realtor Two.

At the same time, Rebecca and William coincidentally began to receive inquiries about the property.

In early July 2014, William telephoned Rebecca to tell her that a neighbor of their lakefront property had telephoned him to tell him that someone had asked about the property.

Rebecca also received a letter from a possible buyer who asked about the property. She returned the telephone call of the potential buyer and advised him to contact Mr. Realtor Two.

Soon after, Mr. Defendant's Attorney emailed Rebecca that he had received an actual offer from a third individual. He would email the appropriate purchase agreement documents to Rebecca for her signature. Rebecca was on her own facilitating the sale of the property.

During a telephone conversation she had with Mr. Defendant's Attorney, he asked her, "Why is all of this falling on you?" Rebecca responded, "I think that the plaintiffs just don't care." It seemed to Rebecca that it was the three plaintiffs' approach to ignore the issue until it went away. It looked as if they didn't care about the consequences.

Chapter XVIII – When Property Could Have Been Listed

Following the January 2013 hearing when Rebecca and William each responded to the judge, The Honorable Mr. Impartial, "I agree to sell the property", the property could have been listed. Both the defendants and Mr. Plaintiffs' Attorney had obtained appraisals by that date. But, the case continued.

Why wasn't the property listed at that time?

Rebecca and William speculated as to a range of possible reasons. First, Mr. Plaintiffs' Attorney had stated that he had an alleged buyer whom he still needed to contact, although he never produced a purchase offer from that buyer. Second, depending on what Mr. Plaintiffs' Attorney told the judge outside of Rebecca's and William's presence, there was a discussion to demolish the property buildings. Third, Rebecca and William awaited further negotiation. Fourth, Rebecca and William believed that an expectation existed as a condition of settlement that they were required to accept Mr. Plaintiffs' Attorney as their attorney and allow him to control the sale of the property. They knew that they were not required to give up their respective shares. Fifth, there remained the apparent expectation that the defendants agree to each pay 1/5 of Mr. Plaintiffs' Attorney's legal fees.

As was the case during the January 2013 hearing, during the October 2013 hearing, Rebecca and William each stated to the judge, this time, The Honorable Mr. Reasonable, "I agree to sell the property." The Honorable Mr. Reasonable ordered that the property be listed. Still the property was not listed for another nine months.

Rebecca's and William's experience is likely not a typical case, however, simply serves as an example of the process of this one partition lawsuit.

Let's review the length of time between each court action for Rebecca's and William's, and their siblings' case.

Chapter XIX – Lengths of Time between Court Actions

1. **Lawsuit filed: 4/23/2012**

2. **Complaint received by defendants: 6/10/2012**
   1 month, three weeks since the lawsuit filing

3. **Pre-Trial Hearing: 9/24/2012** – *3 months, two weeks since the defendants received the complaint*

4. Defendants' Appraisals completed: 11/5-6/2012

5. **Mediation: 11/29/2012** – *2 months, one week since Pre-Trial Hearing*

6. Plaintiffs' Appraisal completed: 12/2012
   (3 months, 1 week since court ordered), (8 months since the plaintiffs filed their lawsuit)

7. **Hearing Two: 1/31/2013** – *2 months since Mediation*

8. **Hearing Three: 4/2/2013** – *2 months since Hearing Two*

9. **Hearing Four: 5/20/2013** – *1 month, two weeks since Hearing Three*

10. **Hearing Five: 10/31/2013** – *6 months since Hearing Four*

11. **Judge Decides Case: 3/6/2014 – *4 months, one week since Hearing Five***

12. New Realtor Selected: 5/7/2014

13. Listing Agreement Sent to Plaintiffs' Attorney: 6/12/2014

14. Plaintiffs Refuse to Sign Listing Agreement: 6/14/2014 (approximately)

15. Defendant Signs Listing Agreement: 7/3/2014

16. **Property Sold: 12/31/2014 – *9 months, three-and-one-half weeks since Judge Decides Case***

Goals of Plaintiffs and Goals of Defendants

Let's also review the assumed goals of the plaintiffs and the goals of the defendants. The plaintiffs filed the lawsuit initially stating that they wanted to sell the property, however, had not discussed anything about their intention or the property with the defendants prior to filing their lawsuit.

Both defendants answered that they agreed to sell the property. One defendant requested that the plaintiffs drop their lawsuit so that the sale could be discussed between the five co-owners amicably and without legal action. The other defendant additionally asked that a Receiver not be appointed so as not to add to potentially costly expenses. Both defendants expressed that the property was particularly meaningful to them as it had been in the family since the 1930s. Also, both defendants asserted that they had attempted to communicate with the plaintiffs and also had begun repair work on the property buildings in actions that benefitted all five co-owners.

The plaintiffs refused to answer any of the defendants' questions pertaining to the sale of the property and the range of situations that could have occurred including sale by auction and foreclosure, both of which could have meant substantial or complete loss of the value of the property to all five co-owners.

The defendants presented an offer to the plaintiffs of $161,000 adjusted to the plaintiffs' three shares based on one of two appraisals that the defendants had obtained. The plaintiffs did not respond to the defendants' offer. Instead, months later, the plaintiffs counter-offered the Competitive Market Analysis amount of $235,000 minutes before a scheduled hearing and without allowing time for Rebecca and William to review documents. Mr. Plaintiffs'

Attorney advised Rebecca that the defendants would have to absorb all of the property taxes. The addition of the taxes would have brought the total to the higher appraisal amount of $250,000. The plaintiffs' attorney also stated that the plaintiffs desired to be compensated based on the expected future decades-from-now value of the property.

The defendants declined to buy-out at the $235,000 plus pay all of the property taxes including those of the plaintiffs.

The judge recommended the appointment of a third appraiser so that a mutual agreed appraisal amount could be determined. Mr. Plaintiffs' Attorney suggested that the appraisers meet to discuss their respective appraisals. The defendants believed that the three appraisers who would meet would be Ms. Low Appraiser ($161,000), Ms. High Appraiser ($250,000), and Mr. Third Appraiser ($250,000). Rebecca and William also were led to believe that the three appraisers would discuss their findings with the defendants so that an amicable settlement could occur.

Mr. Plaintiffs' Attorney instead subpoenaed Ms. High Appraiser, Mr. Third Appraiser, and Mr. Plaintiffs'

Appraiser ($258,000) and informed Rebecca minutes before the hearing that the three latter appraisers would be testifying. He had submitted an Ex-Parte Motion for Adjournment of Trial but didn't advise the defendants if the court had approved his motion or not.

Mr. Plaintiffs' Attorney implied that the plaintiffs would negotiate with the defendants; however in truth he had no intention to negotiate a middle price. His range of negotiation, that he later confirmed, was only a few thousand dollars. The defendants instead viewed a negotiation range as $30,000 to $40,000.

The plaintiffs also sought that the defendants each pay 1/5 of the Plaintiffs' attorney's fees, however Mr. Plaintiffs' Attorney did not tell the defendants what he had billed to date or even his hourly rate. Since the defendants did not agree to share Mr. Plaintiffs' Attorney's fees, the attorney stated to the judge that he would file a motion to award attorney fees and costs to the plaintiffs.

The Honorable Mr. Reasonable warned the defendants that The Honorable Mr. Impartial might rule with the statute that awards attorney fees to the initiator of a lawsuit.

The Honorable Mr. Reasonable did not explain the basis or reasons the ruling might apply.

The Honorable Mr. Impartial ruled that the plaintiffs and defendants would each pay their attorney fees.

Finally, the plaintiffs refused to list the property even though they filed the lawsuit and The Honorable Mr. Reasonable ordered that the property be listed. The plaintiffs also refused to maintain the property or to contribute to repair of the property buildings, specifically roof replacement, therefore allowing the buildings to deteriorate. Without previous discussion with the defendants, the plaintiffs desired that the buildings on the property be demolished. The plaintiffs appeared to prefer that the property be sold at auction or foreclosure resulting in the potential substantial or complete loss of the property's value to all five co-owners. It is unknown if the plaintiffs intended to bid at auction for the property. But according to the rules of the state where the property is located, neither the plaintiffs nor the defendants would have been able to bid as the sellers of the property.

Over two years after the plaintiffs filed the lawsuit, the property was finally listed. The property was not listed immediately after the lawsuit was filed due to court procedures, extended focus on the appraisal amount although no challenges took place, the fact that the lawsuit was filed, and other actions on the parts of the plaintiffs and Mr. Plaintiffs' Attorney.

Chapter XX – Risk of Foreclosure

The Definition of Foreclosure

The definition of tax *foreclosure* (Tax Lien Foreclosure, 2015) is, "The sale of a property resulting from the property owner's failure to pay tax liabilities . . . Properties that are foreclosed due to nonpayment of taxes are deemed tax lien foreclosures . . . Tax laws prevent the former resident of the property (who failed to pay taxes) from bidding at the auction."

Pay the Taxes or Lose Everything if Property Not Sold

Rebecca initially became aware of the property tax billing statements when she received a copy of letter from the person who had been administering her parent's trust and the property of which she was now a co-owner with her four siblings. The letter had been sent to Marta approximately six months before Marta filed the partition lawsuit. Additionally, the letter indicated that each of the other siblings had been mailed a copy. It stated that the co-owners are now responsible for the payment of property taxes. Other documentation that Rebecca later received indicated that Marta had been appointed to receive one tax bill while Debra was to receive the other bill. No one had asked either Rebecca or William to provide input on who should receive the statements.

As had been the case with other issues, neither Marta nor Debra had directly informed Rebecca or William about the property tax bills. To keep informed, Rebecca contacted the trust administrator and the tax assessors for each of the two bills and asked to receive copies of all of the bills. Each tax assessor advised Rebecca that any of the co-owners could obtain a copy of the property taxes at any time simply by requesting that.

But Rebecca thought it important to have regular notification of each tax bill. So, she took it upon herself to have the bills sent to her address. As she received each bill, she sent it to Mr. Plaintiffs' Attorney. When the plaintiffs were no longer represented, Rebecca sent each tax bill to her attorney, Mr. Defendant's Attorney.

As Rebecca began to receive the tax bills, she discussed with William how the five of them could make payments. Rebecca and William agreed that they would suggest that each of the plaintiffs write a check and mail it to Mr.

Plaintiffs' Attorney. Each of the defendants would do the same. Then they proposed that Mr. Plaintiffs' Attorney mail the five checks to the tax assessors. Rebecca presented the plan to Mr. Plaintiffs' Attorney through email. He never responded to her proposal.

Rebecca and William next decided to pay one of the first tax bills. They sent the payment to the tax assessor. Then they requested of the three plaintiffs that they each pay their share of that payment. During mediation, Mr. Plaintiffs' Attorney agreed that the plaintiffs would each pay their share. However, Rebecca and William didn't receive reimbursement from any of their sisters.

As time went on, Rebecca and William regularly asked when and how the plaintiffs would reimburse them for the property taxes that Rebecca and William had paid. Still without receiving a response from Mr. Plaintiffs' Attorney, Rebecca sent a certified letter to each of her sisters advising them of the consequences of failure to pay the property taxes. Marta and Barbara ignored the letter, and both letters were returned unopened by the respective post offices to Rebecca. Debra's letter was accepted; however

Rebecca and William didn't know if she had read the contents.

Rebecca continued to receive the tax bills, and then began to receive delinquent tax notices, and finally received notice of foreclosure statements. Although she forwarded each bill and notice to the attorneys, the plaintiffs did not seem at all concerned. They continued to ignore Rebecca's requests that they respond.

There was a genuine risk of property foreclosure. The state and local governments wanted the payments. Without payment, the reality was that the property could be lost to a sale at auction and possibly with the entire value of the property at stake.

Chapter XXI – Prospective Buyers

Realtor Requires that Plaintiffs Sign Off on Purchase Agreement

The plaintiffs had refused to sign the listing agreement, but Rebecca could sign herself and begin the process to list the property. Mr. Defendant's Attorney sent the appropriate forms to Rebecca to sign. Within a few weeks after she signed the documents, Rebecca saw that the property was listed. The process to list the property took over two years.

Fortunately, approximately three months later a buyer came forward with a formal purchase agreement. But, there were still challenges ahead.

The buyer was not the alleged buyer that Mr. Plaintiffs' Attorney claimed had wanted to purchase the property. Nor was the buyer one of the individuals who had approached Rebecca through letter or William through the neighbors of the property. Rebecca never learned how the buyer became aware that the property was for sale.

No matter though. At least now the process to sell the property could begin. Mr. Defendant's Attorney advised

Rebecca that Mr. Realtor Two had asked him if the plaintiffs still wanted to sell.

Rebecca pondered the question. Yes, the plaintiffs had filed the lawsuit. But the plaintiffs had refused to sign the listing agreement. What did the plaintiffs want? Rebecca felt that she couldn't make an assumption either way and could not speak for individuals who refused to communicate with her. She responded the best that she knew, "I don't know what my sisters want."

Mr. Realtor Two informed Mr. Defendant's Attorney that he required that the three plaintiffs also sign off on the purchase agreement so that the property could be sold.

Thus began a new struggle to attempt to communicate with the plaintiffs who were now without legal representation.

Rebecca gave as much information as she had to Mr. Defendant's Attorney and to Mr. Realtor Two in the form of the email addresses, postal addresses, and telephone numbers she had for her sisters. She also sent emails to her sisters to advise them about the new buyer.

The three plaintiffs ignored Rebecca's emails. The plaintiffs also ignored Mr. Defendant's Attorney's attempts to contact them.

Finally after several weeks, a window of opportunity opened when Barbara suddenly responded to one of Rebecca's emails.

More communication issues existed as both Marta and Debra failed to respond to any emails sent by either Rebecca or Mr. Defendant's Attorney. Barbara mailed one of her signed documents to the surveyor rather than the attorney or the realtor thus requiring a track down of the signed document.

The weeks passed without a response from Marta or Debra. Barbara agreed to contact both of their sisters. Barbara's agreement to cooperate was fortunate because it helped the progress of the sale. One by one, the co-owners signed the listing agreement and began to return the signed purchase agreement with one exception.

In the background, the plaintiffs' attempts to discredit the defendants including the defendants' efforts to sell the property appeared to continue. The realtor praised Barbara while oddly demonstrating distrust toward Rebecca. The plaintiffs apparently persisted in their attempt to control and influence other parties.

Mr. Defendant's Attorney continued to inform Rebecca that not all of the siblings had responded to his emails and letters. He had not received further information from Mr. Realtor Two. Although the two men worked less than two miles from each other, it appeared that Mr. Realtor Two wasn't communicating with Mr. Defendant's Attorney. Rebecca contacted Mr. Realtor Two to inquire if he had all of the necessary signatures yet. Although Mr. Realtor Two stated that he did not have all of the signatures, he cheerfully encouraged Rebecca not to worry. The buyer was very interested, and he had full confidence that the sale would go through. He only awaited Marta's signature. She would be vacationing in Europe, and he wanted to accommodate her schedule.

Marta, the initiator of the lawsuit was the last co-owner to agree to sign the purchase agreement.

Three months later on December 31, 2014, the sale of the property owned by the five siblings was final. They had avoided foreclosure by three months. Thanks to Rebecca's and Mr. Defendant's Attorney's efforts, the property sold. Each of the co-owners was paid one-fifth of the proceeds of the sale minus each of their shares of the property taxes including the plaintiffs' reimbursement of the taxes and insurance that Rebecca and William had paid.

If the case had gotten to foreclosure, could foreclosure have been avoided or would the property have been lost to the five co-owners? That is a question not covered in this book, but for attorneys and judges to answer.

With the sale of the property, Marta's, Barbara's and Debra's partition lawsuit ended.

Rebecca attempted several more times to inquire of Barbara about the wellbeing of their other relatives. She didn't receive a response. The window of opportunity to reestablish relationships had slammed shut again.

A few months later, a stunned Rebecca read on the internet about the recent passing of a close relative. Her relatives had not contacted her about the death. Rebecca shared the news with William. Rebecca and William became the only members of their family of birth who recognized that their once unified family existed. Their siblings and without explanation, all of their other relatives completely stopped communication with Rebecca and William. Rebecca stated, "I guess I was expendable."

Through no fault of either Rebecca or William, their three sisters behaved almost as if the family had never existed. Their extended relatives may have unwittingly participated in a form of mobbing, "they were transformed through three key processes – leveling, sharpening, and assimilation" (Harper, Mobbed, 2013).

Whether due to hatred, indifference, or lack of caring, the loss of family relationships affects all members. The key to facilitating family discussion is the recognition that each co-owner has legal rights despite any disagreement within the family. That other family members respect the rights of other family members can mean the difference between resolving a problem, and finding a solution, or not. Through communication, cooperation, and collaboration, Win-Win solutions can often be found.

Chapter XXII – Attorney Strategies

In legal situations, attorneys play an important role. Lawyers are experts in their respective fields and know the procedures and rules that the court is required to follow. Because legal procedures are by nature adversarial, as is the case with partition lawsuits, tactics that attorneys use may appear to be questionable and extreme in the layperson's perspective. Strategies that appear to have the purpose of influencing a judge, intimidating or discrediting the other party, or earning as much money as possible for the attorney may seem particularly harsh.

Whether due to the attorney's personal style or simply following his or her clients' wishes, attorneys can play a part in establishing either a positive or negative direction that the lawsuit takes depending upon whether he or she encourages or discourages communication and honest direct discussion between each and every co-owner. The attorney's choice of approach may also impact the future level of communication that will occur between members of a family, however likely cannot change individuals who are resolutely determined to refuse to communicate with their relatives.

An attorney's knowledge and display of concern about
the psychological impact of legal action between family
members may not initially seem important. In partition
lawsuits, the legal view is that family conflict is irrelevant
to the judge's decision. However, in an adversarial process
that involves family members, an attorney's accusations,
misstatements and false statements may cause the lawsuit
to take on a life of its own with the focus on a fight rather
than a settlement. While the attorney's client or the
attorney may benefit, the attorney who discourages
communication and instead utilizes biased or manipulated
statements may inadvertently be harming the family as a
unit, let alone individual targets.

Conversely, the attorney who from the outset
demonstrates understanding of the long-term effects that a
lawsuit can have on a family may do the members an
important service simply by recommending face-to-face
honest, sincere discussion prior to filing a lawsuit, and
continuing that approach if the plaintiffs still insist on filing
a lawsuit.

Chapter XXIII – Plaintiffs' Actions

What The Plaintiffs Did Wrong:

Filed the lawsuit without discussion

Refused to drop the lawsuit in favor of non-legal options

Refused direct communication with the defendants

Refused to attend hearings

Weren't honest about their intentions prior to filing lawsuit

Weren't direct about what they wanted after filing the lawsuit, specifically that they intended to refuse to negotiate a middle ground or compromise

Refused to consider creative options toward settlement

Refused to communicate, cooperate, and collaborate

Refused to consider the defendants' points of view

Caused unnecessary delay toward settlement that could have been achieved in two weeks to one month

Refused to contribute toward maintaining the property during the course of their lawsuit

Refused to pay their shares of property taxes leading to unnecessary late fees

Refused to repay the defendants property taxes

Almost forced foreclosure of the property for non-payment of taxes

Attempted to legally force the defendants to pay the plaintiffs' attorney fees

Attempted to coerce the defendants into agreeing to accept the plaintiffs' attorney as their legal counsel

Caused the defendants unnecessary financial waste, the need to hire an attorney, and travel and motel expenses

Initiated a process that caused the defendants emotional and psychological distress

Appeared willing to lose everything through foreclosure rather than compromising with the defendants

What The Plaintiffs Did Right:

Didn't force the appointment of a Receiver

Didn't force the demolition of the property buildings

Chapter XXIV – Defendants' Actions

What The Defendants Did Wrong:

Didn't accept that the plaintiffs refused to negotiate and would not change

Didn't accept that the plaintiffs, prior to filing their lawsuit, had already chosen to dissolve their relationships with the defendants for reasons unknown to the defendants

Didn't understand that the judge would consider only the higher appraisals as the final property value

What Defendants Did Right:

Expressed their love for the property and the history of the property

Remained open to direct discussion with the plaintiffs

Agreed to sell the property

Attempted to communicate with the plaintiffs before and after the plaintiffs filed the lawsuit

Attempted to provide the plaintiffs the opportunity to offer creative options of their own

Created a password-protected website for communication between the five co-owners

Began to pay the property taxes to keep the taxes current

Initiated the mediation

Began repair work on the property buildings

Insured the property

Obtained quotes for roof repair and shared those with the plaintiffs

Forwarded all property tax bills to Mr. Plaintiffs' Attorney

Sent certified mail to the plaintiffs regarding the risk of foreclosure

Sent foreclosure notices to the plaintiffs

Acknowledged personality differences with their siblings

Recognized the need to communicate, cooperate, and collaborate

With the defendant's attorney drove the actual sale of the property

Chapter XXV – Lessons Learned

1. The key to family discussion and unity: communicate, cooperate, and collaborate.
2. A partition lawsuit is an emotionally exhausting and time-consuming process that can take up to two years or longer even when non-contested.
3. Every co-owner has rights as an owner of the property.
4. The individuals who win in a partition lawsuit are the lawyers.
5. The cost of a partition lawsuit depends on the amounts that the attorneys charge and what they bill, the length of the process, and third party fees.
6. Do not file a partition lawsuit as the first option.
7. Do not file a partition lawsuit in a family situation without first discussing non-legal and creative options face-to-face with every co-owner.
8. Negotiation will not be possible with individuals who refuse to meet the other party half-way.
9. Defendants have limited options related to a settlement.
10. Defendants have no control over the length of a lawsuit even when they agree to sell.
11. Be prepared to give up the property once a partition lawsuit is filed. The result of a partition lawsuit is the sale of the property to a third party.
12. Attend all hearings preferably in person.
13. An attorney may attempt confrontational tactics toward the defendants who have been placed in the role simply as relatives of the plaintiffs.
14. Do not take attorney's tactics personally.

15. The plaintiffs' attorney may accuse the defendants of refusing to sell even when the defendants have not contested a sale.
16. Learn legal terms that pertain to partition.
17. Use caution when wording emails.
18. Be prepared to respond objectively to manipulative and deceptive tactics.
19. Seek legal advice before filing documents with the court.
20. Interview multiple attorneys before hiring one.
21. Request a clause in the attorney contract that lists an itemized accounting of all items billed.
22. Request a flat rate when hiring an attorney and ask what the lawyer will do for that rate.
23. Hire an attorney who works within the town in which the property is located.
24. Keep a complete record, both electronic and paper, of all communications, emails, letters, etc.
25. Understand that most appraisers and realtors will be more interested that the property is sold to an outside party than in a buy-out by family members due to the commission that they will earn.
26. Defendants need not obtain appraisals since the plaintiffs' attorney and bank (if a loan is obtained) will obtain one.
27. Develop an agenda listing the specific topics to be discussed prior to the mediation.
28. Delays in a partition lawsuit will result in costing the co-owners more money. Usually only the attorney profits.
29. Keep an accounting of all payments to third parties. Request invoices and proof of payment.
30. Request at least one full week to review documents sent by the plaintiffs' attorney.

31. Request that costs be split by the percentage owned by each co-owner rather than a 50/50 split between the plaintiffs and the defendants.
32. Carefully review every document and have an attorney review before signing.
33. Use caution before agreeing to the opposing attorney's terms.
34. Require that plaintiffs' attorney divulge his final charges before agreeing to pay part of his fees.
35. Do not apply reference to the American Rule without understanding applicable statutes. Seek appropriate legal advice.
36. Copy the plaintiffs' attorney on all communications sent to the judge if not represented by an attorney.
37. A judge makes the final decision about who pays attorney fees.
38. Property taxes are the responsibility of every co-owner depending on the percentage of shares that each owns.
39. Property taxes are paid from the proceeds of the sale of the property when the property sells.
40. All co-owners will handle late fees and penalties of unpaid property taxes based on each co-owner's percentage of shares, or a judge might decide responsibility.
41. If property taxes are not paid, the co-owners including the plaintiffs can lose the entire value of the property to property tax foreclosure.
42. A particular court's process will follow the rules of the state in which the property is located.
43. The process of a partition lawsuit is simply the rules that a judge follows.
44. Attorneys guide the path of a lawsuit.

45. Although a partition lawsuit deals with the division or sale of property, a judge may determine that both the plaintiffs and the defendants are at fault.
46. A partition lawsuit is not only about the sale of property, but more so about the future of family relationships.

Chapter XXVI – Who Won, Who Lost

The question that many ask when learning about partition lawsuits is why would anyone choose to go through such an emotionally charged and costly process?

That question becomes more baffling when family members sue their relatives when the result will essentially be the same with a simple discussion and at significant savings.

This family dispute was based on two opposing perspectives. The defendants approached the situation from the viewpoint of a family needing to work through a problem. The plaintiffs, on the other hand, chose the legal action to force the sale without concern for the future of their sibling relationships.

Regarding the property, the defendants wanted to attempt to save the property since they had not been given that opportunity. The plaintiffs wanted to sell only at the highest appraisal price and would not negotiate or compromise with the defendants. Curiously, the plaintiffs also demonstrated that they were willing to risk foreclosure rather than agree to allow the defendants to purchase the property at a negotiated price.

The sibling' relationships were in a damaged state prior to the plaintiffs' filing of their partition lawsuit. When Marta and Barbara filed the probate action against their parent over a decade earlier also without discussion, they indirectly made a statement about their interest in maintaining the sibling relationships; they sought to end the relationships. Marta and Barbara completely ignored the perspectives of their parent, Rebecca and William while painting them to be villains, but gifted Debra to persuade her to join their alliance.

None of the three plaintiffs told the defendants that they had terminated their relationships nor had they explained their reasons. Rebecca and William believed that their sisters' behaviors were temporary, just part of the ups and downs that are common in interpersonal relationships. The defendants were unaware of any basis for the plaintiffs' decision to end their relationships. However, Rebecca and William knew through court records that the plaintiffs were falsely accusing and characterizing them. Both had been tactics that the three sisters had used throughout their lives even as children.

The plaintiffs' attorney focused on selling the property. At the same time, he attempted to capitalize on the plaintiffs' aggression and acted as an extension of the plaintiffs' methods by implying fault on the parts of the unsuspecting defendants. First, he stated that the defendants refuse to sell, and next he claimed that the defendants challenge the appraisals, among other accusations. Rather than focusing on building on the strengths of the family and preserving relationships, the attorney instead concentrated on emphasizing a contest. In that way, the plaintiffs seemingly justified their actions, and continued their fight.

Their objective appears to have been focused on payment of their attorney fees. It seems that they expected to be awarded all of the proceeds from the sale; they intended that the defendants would lose both of their shares of the proceeds and also be forced to pay the plaintiffs' attorney fees. Therefore, the plaintiffs planned to come out ahead the winners of the contest, suffering no financial loss whatsoever while gaining all of the proceeds from the property's sale.

Had each of the three plaintiffs been honest and straightforward and simply told the defendants in face-to-face discussion their buyer's offer or that they did not really have a buyer, that they did not intend to pay their shares of the property taxes, did not want to be owners, would not negotiate, and were not willing to discuss options to save the property including selling the property to their siblings, the property could have been listed and sold within weeks or months. Filing a lawsuit was not necessary. But, the plaintiffs' explosive, sudden action points to other motives.

Few of the legal participants appeared surprised or alarmed that the plaintiffs' refused to speak directly with the defendants. The act of refusal to communicate was the primary element that determined the course of this legal action. The contest was about a love for money without priority toward preserving the family unit; it was a competition aimed at causing the defendants defeat.

In the case that I've used for an example, there were no winners among the five co-owners. With additional damage done to the family relationships due to their filing of the lawsuit and the plaintiffs' unrelenting animosity, this family's future unity is in continued distress.

The plaintiffs didn't win the contest that they initiated. In the final analysis, the plaintiffs paid Mr. Plaintiffs' Attorney's fees for services that didn't change anything.

Mr. Plaintiffs' Attorney's never shared the results of his final bill with either of the defendants. One can approximate that if his hourly charge was $300.00 per hour, his attendance at only one hearing would calculate to $1500.00 (1 hour to attend hearing, 4 hours of travel). The cost of communications between Mr. Plaintiffs' Attorney and his clients for email and telephone discussions at one hour per week for one year is $15,600. Four hearings at 1500.00 each equal $6,000. Two hearings when Mr. Plaintiffs' Attorney connected by teleconference total $600.00. Add just those amounts together and the result is: $17,700. Add a year for communications with the three plaintiffs and the new total is: $33,300.

$33,300 is a conservative estimate. It is probable that Mr. Plaintiffs' Attorney's charges could have been as high as $50,000 or even higher. The estimate does not include communications that Mr. Plaintiffs' Attorney had with parties other than his clients nor does it include billing for time spent researching and preparing documents, office, and other expenses.

The plaintiffs paid their attorney somewhere between approximately $17,700 and $50,000. If they hadn't filed the lawsuit, their costs would have been minimal. In the end, the plaintiffs lost part of the money that they gained from each of their respective proceeds of the sale.

The plaintiffs expected that the defendants would have to pay the plaintiffs' attorney fees. Fortunately for the defendants, the judge ordered otherwise. But the unspoken damage had already been done. The plaintiffs appeared to intend financial harm to the defendants by attempting to force the defendants to pay for the plaintiffs' actions.

The financial cost to the defendants was also unnecessary. In two years' time, the defendants made the trip to the town where the property is located numerous times for court-related procedures at a cost of thousands of dollars for motel and travel expenses. Although the defendants paid their attorney only a fraction of that which the plaintiffs paid their attorney, Mr. Plaintiffs' Attorney, the hiring of any attorneys wouldn't have been necessary with a simple face-to-face discussion.

Imagine what the money could have gone toward instead of the lawsuit. The plaintiffs could have contributed that money with the defendants to remodel the buildings so that the five siblings could enjoy the property moving forward or to rent the property. The property would have remained a family-vacation property. Or the plaintiffs could have compromised with the defendants to allow them to retain part of the property. Those that no longer wanted to be owners could have made concessions toward family harmony instead of filing a court action.

If the plaintiffs had cooperated with the defendants by developing some creative plan to save the property, the five siblings and each of their families could have continued the legacy of future years as a unified family. The property was a place that the family would go to unite and enjoy one another's company, to discuss the good times and the bad, to support each other, and to share love and kindnesses. Future visits to the property could have helped the siblings to renew relationships and to work through their differences in the neutral space that the property represented.

Property that has been in a family for decades represents different forms of value. It isn't just about the money, but representative of years of shared family memories, activities that go back years since childhood, and experiences with family members who have passed. Those are experiences that are priceless.

The opportunity to renew relationships and the sentimental and nostalgic value of the property can never be matched.

In the end, the individual who profited the most was Mr. Plaintiffs' Attorney as paid by the three plaintiffs at the cost of thousands of dollars.

Mr. Plaintiffs' Attorney's tactics were needlessly aggressive. When the defendants each agreed to sell in The Honorable Mr. Impartial's presence in January 2013, Mr. Plaintiffs' Attorney achieved his goal of forcing sale or partition. It appears that Mr. Plaintiffs' Attorney and the plaintiffs intended more than the sale of the property.

If the plaintiffs had another plan in mind, perhaps to keep the property for the three of them, Rebecca and William never learned. The saddest outcome to Rebecca was that her sisters refused to work together toward a positive conclusion, to Rebecca and William that they save the property.

There are numerous reasons why this lawsuit took over two years to end. Since this was a non-contested lawsuit, one could assume that it should have ended after a few weeks or certainly within a few months. Instead, the case dragged on month after month.

One reason the case lasted for so long was due to the result of opposing interpretations of the goals and objectives of the plaintiffs and the defendants. A second reason were the delays related to Mr. Plaintiffs' Attorney's collection and debate surrounding the appraisals. The third reason came as a result of the plaintiffs' refusal to communicate with the defendants, and Mr. Plaintiffs' Attorney's refusal to encourage each of the three plaintiffs to communicate directly with the two defendants. A fourth reason was Mr. Plaintiffs' Attorney's refusal to respond to Rebecca' and William's questions and the extended lengths of time that he took to respond. There are additional reasons related to court and other legal proceedings.

From the date that The Honorable Mr. Impartial decided the payment of attorney fees to the closing date, an additional ten months had passed.

The total length of the lawsuit from the filing date of April 23, 2012 to the closing date of December 31, 2014 is 2 years, eight months, and eight days. This was a non-contested case.

Author's Final Thoughts

The purpose of this book is to encourage others to carefully and thoroughly consider alternative non-legal options before filling a partition lawsuit, to learn the benefits of family communication, and to understand the range of possible motivations that influence individuals to refuse to communicate with family members.

This book is not only about informing the public about the legal aspects of a partition from a layperson's point of view, the reasons that a partition takes so long to complete, and the challenges that defendants face. It is also about the emotional and psychological aspects of the lawsuit experience.

Though filing a partition lawsuit is not in itself abusive, families may experience irreparable damage as a result of the action. Those that file a lawsuit without communication demonstrate that other issues exist, in some cases that include abusive, bullying behaviors.

Over a decade earlier, two of the three sisters had filed the probate action against their healthy, aging parent without informing their siblings or their parent. During the pre-distribution of their parent's possessions by the plaintiffs, the plaintiffs' ceased their relationships with the defendants. The three sisters in alliance were more motivated to obtain their parent's possessions and property than to maintain their familial-sibling relationships. After their parent's passing almost ten years later, all that remained was the matter of the family-vacation home.

It seems that a love of money, intense anger or hatred, and also an incessant need to control are primary factors that influenced the plaintiffs to file a second legal action and continue it without discussion with the defendants.

The defendants didn't realize that their family of birth no longer existed as a family unit. And they hadn't anticipated that their sisters would use the tactics of manipulation, deception, trickery, and outright lies against them. These were family members.

They also didn't recognize that through the years, their sisters' controlling behaviors had significantly intensified. The group effort caught them off- guard, too. The plaintiffs' alliance widened to include at least one extended relative, who like the three sisters apparently was motivated by money and control.

For every supportive, loving and generous deed that their parent expressed, their sisters demonstrated the opposite extreme, magnified to the most destructive level that seemed possible.

When the plaintiffs cut ties with the defendants, particularly before they initiated their lawsuit, they demonstrated a form of bullying which is a type of emotional abuse. The bullies (plaintiffs) attempted to shame and disgrace their targets (defendants) in an effort to control them (Harper, 2013) and to force compliance. The level of secrecy and the element of surprise that the plaintiffs used against the defendants are also forms of abuse due to excluding the siblings from information and denying them input. Both demonstrate that the plaintiffs desired to ignore and demean the defendants; they wanted absolute control.

There is also an indication that the plaintiffs used the baiting and bashing technique of framing against the defendants. Through their attorneys during the separate legal actions, the plaintiffs attempted to develop a perception of the defendants as villains. Framing is an action in which the "Bully diverts all attention away from his own behavior; the bully seeks support from others, turning them against his target" (Baiting & Bashing, Jan 2014). Individual plaintiffs used *reframing* which means to "challenge the target's view of reality, and *branding*, blaming the target for the target's abuse while at the same time labeling the target as a troublemaker or mentally ill" (Lutgen-Sandvik, 2013) prior to completely terminating communication with the defendants.

Perhaps due to unexplained grudges or apathy, the plaintiffs essentially cast the defendants aside. Despite the defendants' attempts to forgive and renew the relationships, the three plaintiffs continue to refuse communication, likely due to their reluctance to admit fault or responsibility for their actions, and their desire to transfer blame.

Finally, it may be that that unknown issues suddenly developed among one or more of the plaintiffs to influence them to file the lawsuit. However, their refusal to communicate remains a mystery to the defendants.

One might wonder why the defendants would want to continue relationships with individuals who behaved so abusively toward them. The answer lies in the defendants' memories of past constructive, civil, warm, and caring times with their relatives.

But there are only so many times that an individual can forgive others for serious transgressions. When the other persons repeatedly refuse to acknowledge the basic boundaries of respect, regard, and decency, the wise course of action is to move on. Embrace positive, supportive, loyal, and encouraging individuals. Re-evaluate those relationships that impede and suppress.

Until the plaintiffs recognize the defendants' boundaries, and sincerely choose to respect and honor them the same that the plaintiffs demand to be regarded, this family will be troubled. Rebuilding trust is a first step to repairing the siblings' relationships.

Filing a lawsuit has serious consequences. Unfortunately, the law doesn't protect against emotional familial aggression that harms the targets or the consequential damage of a legal action to the family unit.

The extent of damage depends on how much honest communication has taken place between the plaintiffs and the defendants, and the specific behaviors of the plaintiffs as the aggressors up to and during the lawsuit process.

Within the Recommended Resources chapter, the reader will find a list of references that offers a series of scenarios that are related to extreme behaviors and actions, and suggestions to help cope with the abusive behaviors of others. Recognizing symptoms and behaviors can help the reader to locate further information.

In our increasingly litigious society, preparedness offers the best means to protect oneself emotionally and psychologically. The legal process should not be used as a tool to battle and destroy family relationships. There are no safeguards against individuals, even our own family members, who use the legal system in actions against us. Young and older, we are all at risk. Through education, we can help to prepare for the unexpected, protect ourselves and begin to help those who act against us.

I offer these quotes and final thoughts.

For those who seek spiritual guidance, what better resource to suggest than the Bible.

"Love of money is the root of all evil" (The Bible, 1 Timothy 6:9 - King James Version - 1 Timothy 6:11 - New International Version).

We each need money to survive. However, when the love of money becomes more important than valuing relationships with family members, the result are behaviors that hurt others, our loved ones.

"Let all bitterness and wrath and anger and clamor and slander be put away from you, along with all malice. Be kind to one another, tenderhearted, forgiving one another, as God in Christ forgave you" (The Bible, Ephesians 4:31-32 - English Standard Version).

These words strengthen and guide toward building positive relationships.

"In your core value, you will act with conviction to achieve fairness, which is likely to be in your long-term best interests. In anger you will devalue others - at least in your head - which is unlikely to be in your long-term best interests" (Stosny, 2008).

A complicated subject, the topic of anger involves a multitude of levels and aspects. Among those are: projection, feelings of entitlement, holding grudges, and blaming others (Namka, 2002). At one end of the spectrum, anger is a valid emotion when controlled. However, when uncontrolled even as a sub-level through either rage or suppression, the end result can still be destructive with harm to the bearer and to his target.

Many unsuspecting targets particularly those who report aggressors' offenses while attempting to self-protect are inaccurately labeled as feeling anger or are accused of being bullies themselves. However, those who are, in reality, responsible are often the aggressors who refuse to acknowledge their own anger and instead project it on their targets. When the targets are subsequently blamed for their aggressors' emotions and actions, interpretation of who holds responsibility for the anger and aggression becomes more multifaceted. As the aggressors further attempt to contort the truth while claiming righteousness, they cause potential and likely intended greater harm to their targets.

"For the person with a high need for control, the dominant characteristic is not wisdom, but fear…" (Neill, 2015).

Being in control and controlling others is not the same. The former describes an individual with a healthy emotional and psychological state of wellbeing. The latter is representative of a "controlling personality who probably has deeper issues, such as codependency, narcissism, sociopathic tendencies or just sheer stubbornness" (How to Recognize a Controlling Person, 2015).

Hough (April, 2014) described control this way: "Control doesn't mean having the final say or always having things your own way. In a fair and equal society, control means sharing power and resources, entering into debate and negotiation, having your voice heard and valued, and having the same chances as everyone else."

Finally, I want to emphasize the primary lessons learned that can make a tremendous difference in preserving family relationships.

For some, perhaps also, your property can be saved.

Don't file a partition lawsuit. Discuss. Communicate. Cooperate. Collaborate.

Chapter XXVII – Recommended Resources

Contact a licensed attorney with expertise in partition law in the state where the property is located with questions and for further information about the partition lawsuit process.

I suggest the book, *Healing from Family Rifts: Ten Steps to Finding Peace After Being Cut Off From a Family Member* by Mark Sichel. This book offers case studies that describe the experiences of individuals whose families have dissolved relationships with them. It is important to note the author's descriptions that the individuals are themselves not at fault for the actions that their families took. Through case studies, the reader can learn to accept that he or she is not to blame for the actions of others. Individuals may never know why their relatives demonstrate aggression against them, and it is likely that they did nothing to cause the relatives' aggression. Mr. Sichel describes the behaviors of individuals that range from mild aggression to personality disorders and severe mental health issues.

One of many resources that describe the problem of adult bullying is *Adult Bullying* by Pamela Lutgen-Sandvik,

Ph.D. The author has taken her scholarly study and edited it for non-scientific audiences. Although the author discusses bullying in a workplace context, the parallels of negative acts to abusive sibling relationships include, "Had information withheld, had your opinions ignored, been humiliated or ridiculed, had gossip spread about you, been ignored, excluded, or isolated from others, experienced intimidation with threatening behaviors with invasion of personal space, and had false allegations made against you" (Lutgen-Sandvik, 2013).

Jay Carter, Psy. D. focuses on the topic of invalidation in his book *NASTY People.* With descriptions of the "methods of uncertainty, projection, generalization, judgment, manipulation, sneak attack, double message, cutting communication, building you up, cutting you down, and the double bind" (Carter, 2004), the author offers ways that the invalidator's target can cope.

Dealing with People You Can't Stand by Dr. Rick Brinkman and Dr. Rick Kirschner recommends ways to deal with difficult people and suggests ways to communicate toward cooperative solutions.

I recommend the book, *Almost a Psychopath* by Ronald Schouten, MD, JD, and James Silver, JD. Also through case studies, the authors describe the various factors that influence behaviors and how to deal with individuals who commit offenses that hurt others without feelings of empathy. Numerous mental health issues may be influential factors. Those that are commonly related to family dysfunction include narcissism ("a lack of empathy, the need for absolute control, the action of provoking an argument and then blaming the target, a strong sense of entitlement, being exploitative of others, and arrogant attitudes") (Narcissism, PsychCentral, 2015) and antisocial behavior ("a disregard for the feelings of others, a lack of remorse or shame, manipulative behavior, unchecked egocentricity, and the ability to lie in order to achieve one's goals") (Antisocial Personality Disorder, PsychCentral, 2015). Alcohol and substance abuse may also be issues.

Many families can be saved, and partition lawsuits perhaps avoided by following these most basic common sense rules. GodFruits.com listed those as: "Always be honest, Count your blessings, Forgive and forget, Be supportive of one another, Be kind and tenderhearted, Keep your promises, Comfort one another, and above all, Love one another" (Family Rules, 2015).

For the reader interested in learning more about the psychological aspects of dealing with the negative behaviors of others, there are a multitude of resources available on the internet.

Finally, to researchers, educators, and other scholars, I propose the topic of rejection by family members as an element of a partition lawsuit to learn more about the challenges that present to families and especially individual family members.

References

American Rule. (2015). Retrieved from
http://www.investopedia.com/terms/a/american-rule.asp

American Rule (attorney's fees). (2015). Retrieved from
https://en.wikipedia.org/wiki/American_rule

Antisocial Personality Disorder Symptoms. (2015).
Retrieved from
http://psychcentral.com/disorders/antisocial-
personality-disorder-symptoms/

Appraisal. (2015). Retrieved from
http://www.investopedia.com/terms/a/appraisal.asp

Arbitration and Mediation. (2015). Retrieved from
http://adr.findlaw.com

Baiting & Bashing. (Jan, 2014). Retrieved from
https://psychopathresistance.wordpress.com/2014/01/13
/baiting-and-bashing/

Carter, Jay, Psy.D. (2004). *NASTY People.* NY, NY:
McGraw-Hill.

Collett, Marsha L., Esq. (March, 2011). *What Is A Right of
First Refusal?* Retrieved from
http://www.wickenslaw.com/firm-newsletter-
archive/what-is-a-right-of-first-refusal/

Discovery. (2015). Retrieved from
http://dictionary.law.com/Default.aspx?selected=530

Evidence. (2015). Retrieved from
http://dictionary.law.com/Default.aspx?selected=671

Exhibit and Witness Lists. (2015) Retrieved from
https://definedterm.com/exhibit_and_witness_lists

Family Rules. (2015). Retrieved from
https://GodFruits.com

Folberg, Jay (Dec, 2009). *Mediating Family Property and Estate Conflicts: Keeping the Peace and Preserving Family Wealth.* Retrieved from http://mediate.com

Harper, Janice, Ph.D. (2013). *Mobbed! A Survival Guide to Adult Bullying, and Mobbing.* Retrieved from
http://www.amazon.com/Mobbed-Survival-Guide-Bullying-Mobbing-ebook/dp/B00ERMBY84

Harper, Janice, Ph.D. (Sep 17, 2013). Bullying, Mobbing and the Role of Shame. Retrieved from
https://www.psychologytoday.com/blog/beyond-bullying/201309/bullying-mobbing-and-the-role-shame

Hedges, Kristi (Dec, 2013). *Six Surprising Negotiation Tactics That Get You The Best Deal.* Retrieved from
http://www.forbes.com/sites/work-in-progress/2013/12/05/six-surprising-negotiation-tactics-that-get-you-the-best-deal/

Hough, Juliette (Apr 28, 2014). Being in control matters – for everyone [Web log post]. Retrieved from
http://www.neweconomics.org/blog/entry/being-in-control-matters-for-everyone

How, and How Much, Do Lawyers Charge? (2015).
  Retrieved from http://research.lawyers.com

How to Recognize a Controlling Person. (2015). Retrieved
  from http://www.wikihow.com/Recognize-a-
  Controlling-Person

Levy, Robert I. (2014). ADR (Alternative Dispute
  Resolution) and Mediation. Retrieved from
  http://www.businessandrealtylaw.com/2014/06/11/adr-
  alternative-dispute-resolution-and-mediation/

Lutgen-Sandvik, Pamela, Ph.D. (2013). *A Nasty Piece of
  Work: Translating a Decade of Research on Non-
  Sexual Harassment, Psychological Terror, Mobbing,
  and Emotional Abuse on the Job.* St. Louis, MO:
  ORCM Academic Press.

Namka, Lynne, Ed. D. (2002). *Projection, Blaming,
  Grudge Holding, Doomsday Thinking, Revenge
  Thoughts, Black and White Thinking: Irrational Ways
  of Thinking Which Keep You Angry.* Retrieved from
  http://www.angriesout.com/grown14.htm

Narcissistic Personality Disorder Symptoms. (2015).
  Retrieved from
  http://psychcentral.com/disorders/narcissistic-
  personality-disorder-symptoms/

Neill, Neil, Ph.D. (2015). *The Paradox of the Need to
  Control.* Retrieved from http://www.neillneill.com/the-
  paradox-of-the-need-to-control

Partition. (2015) Retrieved from
  http://TheFreeDictionary.com;

Partition. (2015). Retrieved http://partition.uslegal.com

Partition of Heirs Property Act Summary. (2015).
Retrieved from http://www.uniformlaws.org

Partition (law). (2015). Retrieved from
http://Wikipedia.com

Pretrial Conference. (2015). Retrieved from http://legal-
dictionary.thefreedictionary.com/Pretrial+Conference

Schouten, Ronald, MD, JD, & Silver, James, JD. (2014).
Almost A Psychopath. Center City, Minnesota:
Hazelden.

Sher, Malcolm. (2010, April). *Emotional and Technical
Challenges to Mediating Partition Actions.* Retrieved
from http://www.mediate.com/articles/sherM3.cfm

Sichel, Mark. (2004). *Healing from Family Rifts: Ten Steps
to Finding Peace After Being Cut Off From a Family
Member.* NY, NY: McGraw-Hill.

Stosny, Steven, Ph.D. (Dec, 2008). *Anger Problems: What
They Say about You.* Retrieved from
https://www.psychologytoday.com/blog/anger-in-the-
age-entitlement/200812/anger-problems-what-they-
say-about-you

Summons and Complaint (2012). State of Michigan,
Judicial Circuit.

Tax Lien Foreclosure (2015). Retrieved from
http://www.investopedia.com/terms/t/tax-lien-
foreclosure.asp

Transcript (2015). Retrieved from http://legal-dictionary.thefreedictionary.com/transcript

Trial Brief (2015). Retrieved from http://dictionary.findlaw.com/definition/trial-brief.html

The Serenity Prayer

"God grant me the serenity to accept the things I cannot change; courage to change the things I can; and wisdom to know the difference."

Reinhold Niebuhr

Author Biography

Stephanie Siddall Germack earned her Ph.D. in Psychology from Walden University. She is also a graduate of Roosevelt University, the Otis Art Institute of the Parsons School of Design, and the University of Cincinnati. Based on her wide range of experience, Dr. Germack is devoted to building awareness about the many issues that affect families.

Other books by Stephanie Siddall Germack Ph.D., NCC, LPC

Attitudes and Knowledge of Aging and Dementia among Legal and Medical Professionals (2012)
Available from ProQuest Dissertations

Legal and Financial Exploitation of our Elders (2007)

NOTES